From Akenfield to Pastures New

Peggy Cole MBE

"For Eileen"

LUCAS BOOKS
www.lucasbooks.co.uk

From Akenfield to Pastures New

First Published by
LUCAS BOOKS 2008

ISBN 978- 1903797-87-7

British Library Cataloguing in Publication Data
A catalogue record for this book is available from the British
Library

Printed in the UK by PrintWright Ltd.

Mixed Sources
Product group from well-managed
forests and other controlled sources
www.fsc.org Cert no. SGS-COC-004573
© 1996 Forest Stewardship Council
FSC

CONTENTS

'Akenfield' today

The author wishes to thank Audrey Bugg, Russell Cole, Sarah Cole (for her understanding and translating from Suffolk into English), Beverley Gugenheim, John Lucas, Terry Mott and Roy Tricker for their help with this book.

FOREWORD

For over twenty years now I have enjoyed being a friend of Peggy Cole. We met back in the 1980s when our first books were published and I (like H.R.H. Princess Margaret and thousands of others) was taken to see her amazing Charsfield council house garden, which was featured on Gardener's World. What really sticks in my memory from this visit was the huge hug that she gave me to send me on my way. Peggy has generated thousands of pounds for charity and she has brought untold happiness to countless people through her books, her broadcasts, her weekly articles in the East Anglian Daily Times and through her amazing output of lectures and demonstrations, in this country and far beyond.

Above all, Peggy lives and breathes the Suffolk countryside and is proud to be a 'Suffolk Mawther' - born and bred! An acknowledged expert in horticulture, cookery, winemaking and other skills, also a star in the nationally-acclaimed film Akenfield, and the recipient of a well-deserved M.B.E., Peggy will always be the Country Girl at Heart that she presents to us in her first book. In her company you get straight Suffolk talk, Suffolk wit, genuine Suffolk dialect, scrumptious Suffolk hospitality, a wealth of stories and a deep insight into what makes real people 'tick'. And this is also what radiates through her writing.

This book tells of the latest chapter in Peggy's eventful life, when she leaves her beloved Charsfield to make a new beginning in her bungalow in Melton, surrounded by her vast library of books, collections of postcards and mouthwatering ephemera! Although arthritis makes walking difficult for her, her 'retirement' stills provides plenty of writing and lecturing. She does now find more time to read and to discover lovely out-of-the-way Suffolk villages and churches which fascinate her.

"I consider myself lucky", she recently told me. Indeed so are we, her friends and admirers, to have this latest product of her pen and so to enjoy another helping of this much-loved Suffolk Mawther's insight, wit, common-sense and superb storytelling.

Roy Tricker
Eastertide 2008

Chapter 1

A Kindly Push

I wonder how many of you remember my first book, '*A Country Girl at Heart*', or the revised edition? If so, you will have seen that I was hoping to be able to stay in my last home, Akenfield in Charsfield, until I ended my journey in this life. But this was not to be. As I tell my many friends, "we never know what is round the corner and it's best to take one day at a time." I would never have thought that I would have had to move house but with my ill health I think it was meant to be. For years I have suffered with arthritis and also I have had bad ulcers on my legs. As I get older it seems to get worse.

I shall never forget my sons coming to see me and telling me in July 2001 that the garden was getting too much to look after. I know my brother had been very good doing all the hard work but, as my sons explained to me, it was not fair to expect him to do this with his other jobs as well. "Have an easier time for the rest of your life," they said, "we will put your house on the market."

"Oh no," I said, "I can't leave here. Where will I put all my bits and pieces?"

After they left I sat down and had a good cry. No, I thought, I can't move. But within three to four days my eldest son rang to tell me that he had been in touch with an estate agent who would be calling to look at my house in a day or two. I couldn't believe it. I think I was crying on and off all week. I had been living in Charsfield for 41 years and my garden had been visited by thousands of people from all over the world. My son had found me a bungalow in Melton not far from his home.

"Be ready on 26th July, as I will pick you up at about 3.30pm to have a look," he told me. I couldn't believe how quickly everything was moving. It made me realise I really was on the move!

My son and daughter-in-law collected me. We met the estate agent and looked at the bungalow. It had three bedrooms, a lounge, kitchen, small pantry cupboard, shower room, toilet and airing cupboard with an attached single garage. I looked round and my son asked "Will it do you, Mum?"

"Yes, it will do me" I replied.

The bungalow was lovely and clean and in good order throughout. There was a nice little garden with a small pond, shrub borders and lawns. I remember that day my leg ulcer was giving me hellish pain. I felt awful. I asked my son how he had seen that this place was for sale. It was on a small estate with houses and bungalows. He had put a note through the letter boxes of all the bungalows asking the occupants if they wanted to sell and if so would they give him a ring? As luck would have it, my neighbour who knew him gave him a ring and told him that the lady who had lived in what was to be my new home had gone into a home so her family had just put the property on the market. I was very lucky. My son put an offer in and this was accepted within a week. I then realised that I was going to move and this was certain! My family had got it in mind that I should have an easier life.

Now if I can just say that moving house after having lived in a place for a life time is as bad as suffering a bereavement. I had heard people say this before but I had just put it to the back of my mind and until you have to do it you don't know what they are talking about really. As I went to bed that night after looking at the bungalow, I watched a barn owl flying down the field opposite my windows and thought, "God, I am going to miss all this countryside and the country lanes". I then thought about what my brother was going to say as I had been giving him his meals since my husband had died in May 1980. My mother had died in 1978 so Ronnie had spent his time helping me while I looked after him but he still had his own bungalow. He was very quiet when I told him I was moving and he said that I must do what I thought best.

This was not a move that had been planned for months. I had already booked my table for preserves at the Wantisden weekend. They used to run the '*Power of the Past*' weekend for the St. Elizabeth Hospice. It was like a smaller version of the Suffolk Show. For months I had been busy making preserves so I already had jars full of jams,

Hard life behind a team of Horses

marmalades and pickles ready for the September and December shows. My brother used to cut up so much of the fruit and vegetables in the evening and, of course, the garden was full of vegetables and fruit. As it became fit and ripe I used it. I have been brought up not to waste anything. That's what the war years did for us.

So in between cooking preserves I began to pack. "Where do I start?" I thought. Firstly, I had four sheds and two greenhouses to clear. I had so many garden tools. Some were given to my late husband; these included old sugar beet forks and sugar beet toppers, cross cut saws and even a hay knife which was used to cut the old hay stakes. We also had hay rakes, three or four spades, jars and jars full of old nails and screws (you never know, one might come in handy!), boxes of old door hinges, reap hooks and 'flashers', which were used to cut wood and sticks. This was what my brother and I called 'Ernie's shed'. My late husband had worked on the land and was a grave digger so he had his own tools including wedges, axes, slashers and bill hooks; all tools for wood cutting which was done a lot in the country when we had open fires. Ernie used to thatch so he also had his old thatching tools. On the shed bench were brace and bits, chisels, small hammers and a cobbler's foot; useful if rubber heels came off your shoes. Under the bench lay sickles, a sledge hammer, pick axe and also the Adze, a useful tool for pulling old roots out of the ground. Tins of old paint were there plus paint brushes, bags of old string and boxes of sundries we used for the garden. Yes, it was like a small museum. I had a good friend who came with his lorry and took a lot of the tools to a local sale yard. Some went to *'Tools with a Mission'*; they came and collected them and took them to an old barn where a group of people repaired them, then they were sent to help people in developing countries. I could not believe what had come out of that shed. Another good friend got me two skips so the rubbish was put in them as we cleared it out.

The next shed was where my home-made wine and equipment for making the wine were kept. I had about 80 gallons of wine, the best I had put into bottles to keep for the Over 60's Christmas Lunch. I had been doing this for many years. I gave a lot of the equipment away then I put so many bottles, demijohns, tops and air locks into the skip (how I wish I had hung on to some of these as later I had to go and buy some more - more on that shortly!). I also had a dozen or so plastic buckets, a large fruit rack and the roof was covered with hanging dried flowers and many old baskets. (I may add they were also filled with bottle tops, etc.) For years I had done flower arrangements in churches and at shows. I gave many of the items away but, once again, I have had to buy some more flower containers since moving. I am sure readers will know all about this if they have moved. My big chest freezer was also in my 'wine shed' as I called it so each day I was trying to make something with the fruit - the lady who bought my house also bought the freezer and the chickens so I did not have to worry about them but I do miss my fresh eggs!

The next shed was at the top of the garden where we used to keep chicken food and spare tables for when I used to have cheese and wine parties in the orchard. I also had dozens of seed trays and boxes, hanging baskets and greenhouse equipment which I stored in the shed when not in use: rolls of plastic, fleece, straw, canes and lawn mowers, even village games which we stored for the local fêtes. I had hundreds of flower pots which I gave away or put into the skip.

Sometimes when I wanted to think I would make a cup of tea and go and sit on the seat near the fish pond. I called it my 'bolt hole' where I could rest quietly. I had a lot to think about. My sister Eileen had died on July the 10th from cancer. She was only 56 and had been ill for just about eight weeks. I shall never forget how kind the staff at the St. Elizabeth Hospice were to us all. I had also lost two more friends from the same illness in the last few weeks and was wondering where it would all stop. But when you have been a widow for so long I think you are given extra strength to get on with life.

The next big job was cleaning out the loft and, being a hoarder, I had so many black bags full of old newspapers, some dating back years, plus gardening magazines, old Christmas cards, in fact all sorts of things. My sons came and collected the bags and brought them out to me in the garage. As I went through them I told my sons, "I must keep this, I must keep that". "No, Mum," they said and put them in the skip. I tried to get some out but I could not reach. I decided to have a garage sale and put an advert in the paper to give the time of the sale, 10am - 4pm. At 9am people were starting to arrive but it was not the garage they were interested in, it was the skips! People were trying to climb in. I looked on in amazement. They were taking old picture frames, shopping baskets, flower pots, all sorts went out of that skip (how I wish I had taken a photo). Some of my furniture I donated to the battered wives' home and I gave away a lot of bed linen and towels as I had seen that Bosnia was in need of all sorts of blankets, etc.

Next came the packing of my books. My sons still laugh and say their backs have never been the same since they moved those boxes of books. I sold ten book cases so you can guess how many I had to get rid of. I took 16 boxes to charity shops and gave a lot away. I still have many books; I just love them and will tell you about them later. I also had all my photo albums and 48 boxes and rings of transparencies (for years I had gone round giving illustrated talks). A friend came and helped me to pack my books as some were old and fragile. In the meantime the TV and press had been round to do some articles about the garden and to ask why I was selling up. Sometimes these reporters asked daft questions. They were the last people I wanted to talk to.

The estate agent had been and put up a For Sale board. That was when it hit me - "No going back, my girl" I thought and then we started to have the first lot of people round. I tried to keep the place as tidy as possible but people do understand why there are boxes, etc. Some came with no intention of buying but I am told by friends that you get this when a house goes on the market.

By the first week in August I had the first couple come to view the house. After that more people visited. Some thought the garden was too big or the house too small. In the meantime I had the press coming to take photos of the garden and the front of the house. Then BBC television came to take pictures and to do a write-up on the garden. I should have expected this as it had been a well-known garden to visit for the last twenty-eight years and people had come from all over the world. Many times I had six to eight coaches of visitors a week. The church ladies used to do cream teas for the visitors and raise money for church funds and the evening coach loads would have a Ploughman's Supper, made by the local village Women's Institute so they were able to boost their funds.

Some people who pick this book up to read it may wonder what the Women's Institute is. It all started in Stoney Creek, Ontario, Canada in 1897 and soon spread fast. By the year 1902 there were thirty-six Institutes and 3000 members had joined. One can understand that there were not many socities for women to join at that time and this was a way of getting together. I understand that Mrs Alfred Watt, a founder member of the Metchosin Institute, travelled to London and attended a conference on industrial and agricultural cooperation. England was at war so it had become vital that farming should prosper and that food should be grown at home and brought to the great city markets. From this meeting Mrs Watt began to tell her story of the Women's Institute Movement in her country and its cooperative ideals. The rest of the committee must have thought this was a good idea as the first Women's Institute was formed in Bangor, Wales, on 11 September, 1915. As it was wartime, the women in all parts of the country felt they would like to help in some way. Soon they were working on the land, growing and picking daffodils, narcissi and tulips, egg collecting and sending these to the town markets. Then came blackberry picking. These were sent to London for jam making (I suppose this is where jam and Jerusalem came in as the W.I. has for many years had a tradition of jam making). Each W.I. has a committee and meets once a month with speakers giving interesting talks. Years ago it must have been a real treat for so many women who lived miles apart to come and meet and learn about a range of interesting subjects. The main purpose of the Institute was to improve and develop the conditions of rural life. The Chairman of the National Federation of Women's Institutes was Lady Denman, CBE. She was a wonderful woman to the W.I. and she did everything in her power to help the women of her country with education and in other ways, too many to list. A college was purchased in 1947 called Denman College, where W.I. members can go to learn new subjects and develop their skills. I went with a friend and we had a lovely time learning all about preserve making. You meet other members from all over the country. Yes, the W.I. has come a long way and may it go from strength to strength. There is so much more I could say but if there is a W.I. near you, go along. I am sure you will be made welcome and you can always learn something new.

In the meantime the garden was producing so many wonderful vegetables and fruit. I wanted to use up as much as I could so there was not a day went by when I was not making jams, wine, pickles or preserves of some sort as this had been my way of life for years. I do hate waste so I would make use of any vegetable or fruits going spare. Visitors would often ask me if they could taste some wine or buy a pot of home-made jam.

From Akenfield to Pastures New

For years I have been a member of the Women's Institute so have had to take my Hygiene Certificate and refresher course over the years, which all members have to take if they cook for Women's Institutes. People who cook or have anything to do with food have to take a food hygiene course. The rules have been much updated in the last few years. Even village halls have rules where two or three sinks have to be in use. When I think that we used to have just a washing up bowl and bucket of water in our village hall! So much has changed over the years . I know it's nice to have the water plumbed in and a sink to use but some of the rules don't help much.

When you talk about home-made wine some people look at you and say that with the materials and equipment required, it's too much trouble to make. But it's like everything; if you enjoy making wine, carry on. You don't have to have expensive equipment. Most of the things you need are probably already there in your kitchen. For all my wine making I used an earthenware pan that was my mother's and a large white plastic bucket. Then you will need a funnel, plastic ones are the cheapest. Never use anything tinny or iron-based as an unpleasant flavour can be imparted to the wines. Aluminium or glass will do. You will also need a large jug and muslin for straining the wine (I used a fine old piece of net curtain which answered the purpose very well). Sadly, home-made wine making has gone out of fashion in the last fifteen years or so and I have seen so much wine equipment at car boot sales. I am told that many people go over to the Continent and get wine cheaply while on holiday.

However, back to basics. You will need to invest in a demijohn (but these I have seen in charity shops). You will also need a bung and air lock plus a wooden spoon with a piece of plastic tubing to siphon the wine from the demijohn, a few Campden tablets and yeast and sugar. One tip I would give is never put all the sugar in to the wine. When making

14

a gallon, the recipe will say 3 to 3½ lbs sugar but often I would get a very sweet wine so I used to cut it down to 2½ lbs. You can always add sugar but you can't take it out.

Once you start making wine, think how often you will be able to enjoy the fruits of your labour and not only you but your friends too. And there is a lot to be said for swapping tips and ideas over a glass of wine! You do need to keep it at a temperature of 65 F (18 C); this is easy in summer but not so easy in winter. I have heard of friends of putting theirs in an airing cupboard; that's fine if you have a big enough airing cupboard! Always keep your wines covered with a lid or thick cloth in the early stages before the wine goes into the demijohn otherwise you will be plagued with small flies (brown or black) and if they get to your wine they will turn it sharp and sour, like vinegar (I always call them vinegar flies). Make sure your containers are clean and free from any bacteria. Sterilize them using six Campden tablets in a pint of water (this mixture can be used again and again before you discard it). Once a bottle of home-made wine has been opened it will keep indefinitely, unlike bought wines. Also all wines improve with keeping. Always be sure that your wine is cool but not cold when adding the yeast. I first learnt wine making in the late sixties going to the Felixstowe and then the Kesgrave Wine Circles. At one time at the wine shows there would be 500 bottles of wine to be judged! One year at Felixstowe I got best in the show with a rose petal wine I had made from the '*Fragrant Cloud*' rose. It was a lovely deep red colour. There is no need to pick the roses at their best but when they are just about to fall (so you are saving them from the compost heap). I had a bucket full of petals, 3lbs sugar, 1 lemon, 1 orange, a handful of raisins. Put the rose petals in a wine making vessel and pour over the boiling water. Stir well, cover and then leave for 2-3 days before straining and adding the chopped raisins, the juice from the lemon and orange and the sugar. Stir well, sprinkle on the yeast and leave covered for two more days. Then strain, pour into a demijohn and leave for six months, more if you can wait! My other favourite wines were apricot, blackberry, cherry, damson, dandelion, gooseberry, oak leaf, orange, sloe, wheat and so on. Many of the visitors to my garden when it was open loved to look at my wine shed and wanted to buy a bottle. But you can't sell home-made wine; you have to have a customs licence. However, I used to have some good parties in the summer for charity and Ronnie would help me to get the wine out to the orchard. How some people walked home I don't know! It was very strong and powerful, much stronger than wine you buy in shops, which caught some people out! One couple fell into a ditch on their way home. I always laugh about my home-made wine nights. Ronnie would keep an eye out for the first oak leaves (as they had to be young) and also the first dandelions. Then he would pick them and help to get the flowers or fruit ready. My kitchen used to smell like a brewery!

However, back to clearing my wine shed. Most of the wine had been bottled up but I knew I could not take it all with me. I had shelves on which I had stored all sorts of things over the years, such as baskets and boxes of plates as I often had cheese and wine parties in the garden and orchard. Another job I had always done at the end of August was to plant up a hundred hyacinth bulbs to flower for Christmas as I would give them out for Christmas presents and also sell them at W.I. markets. I ordered them in May so that was another job to fit in. I don't expect many people have moved house and taken five trays of bowls and pots of hyacinths with them and of course they have to be in a dark, cold place until four weeks before Christmas. My sons did not say much to me about them but it was all extra lifting for them. On the Bank Holiday Sunday we had a lady come round and she made an offer for the house which we accepted. She was a gardener and a single parent. The next day she returned and told me she would like to build on to the house (which she later did).

I didn't have much sleep for the next few days as I

knew now that I would be leaving the village. I was Chairman of the Parish Council at that time so at the next meeting I had to give in my notice. I felt rather sad about it as I had enjoyed the work and all that it had entailed. I also had some village shows to judge in September and I was on other committees too. I had friends round at weekends so I was able to give them apples and plums. In the meantime my son arranged for a survey to be done on the bungalow that I was going to buy. There are so many papers to fill in or sign and they go back and forth between solicitors. You wonder why it takes so long.

The new owner-to-be of my house wanted me to leave the cooker and washing machine. That was handy as I was buying the same from the owners of the bungalow where I was going. It avoided a lot of lifting and undoing of wires, etc.

It was now the second week in September. I was still making preserves ready for my stall at the end of the month at the Power of the Past show. I remember I was sitting at the table peeling apples and the date was September the 11th. I had just put the television on and thought I would like to see what the afternoon film was about. Sometimes if they were the old black and white films made in 1930-40 I would video them to watch later. As I looked at the television, I saw an aeroplane hit one of the Twin Towers in Manhattan, USA. Then another one, with balls of fire. I could not believe that what I was watching was real; I really did think it was a film. I was just about to switch off the television when I heard a commentator say it was a crash and that was the start of terrorism as we know it. What a lot has happened since that awful day.

When I saw the two planes crashing in to the Twin Towers in Manhattan, New York, I could not help thinking of my first visit there in 1987. I was on a lecture tour and was to give a talk at the English Speaking Union. Friends I was staying with took me on a tour to see all the famous places of interest. I remember looking up at the Twin Towers. My friends said we could go up if I wanted to as there were only 92 floors! I declined the offer but did go in on the bottom floor to look around. I still think of this disaster every time I see photos and old films which show the towers in the background. I bought a large set of postcards showing the different stages of the fires and the building coming down. I am sure the American people will never forget this apocalypse. When you think that between 40,000 and 50,000 people went to work in the Twin Towers each day. There were reported to be 20,000 inside when the planes hit the towers. At morning rush hour, the famous towers stood tall, clean, elegant and familiar; steel hallmarks of the city's skyline. An hour later they had vanished, burying and crushing huge crowds below and bringing down with them thousands of panic-stricken workers stranded on stairs or in their offices. Fire escapes were gnarled and twisted.

As one secretary said, "There were so many people running down the stairs, running over each other and screaming and pushing and trying to get out."

Some on the 92nd storey would never have got out another lady said.

The planes' hijackers had succeeded where the bombers of 1993 had failed. The air cleared over where the twin towers of the World Trade Centre had once stood. As another woman said, "I can't imagine what an atomic bomb is like but maybe this is it. This is an amazingly traumatic day for our country." We in England had suffered in the war when buildings came down and so many people were killed. But the Americans had never seen anything like this. As one nurse said, "This is what hell looks like, in case you'd ever stopped to wonder." I have always thought that war is awful but now we have terrorism, worse in many ways because you never know when they will strike next.

Whilst getting on with my packing and continuing to

make my preserves I used to try and have a rest in the middle of the day and put my feet up as my ulcers were still painful although they were healing. I must say the pain can be so terrible, just like a bad toothache gnawing away but you get used to it. I had started to take cuttings or split up plants and put them into smaller pots - just a few as I had had orders from my son not to take many as they would need watering. Also I had a lot of patio pots planted which I had already put by to take with me. I had sold some big pots with plants in which were a few years old.

The weekend came for me to take my preserves to Power of the Past at Wantisden. Allan and my grandson Russell brought their cars and we took my car as well, full up! It was a busy weekend and over 600 jars of preserves were sold. It is just like the Suffolk Show with plenty of people. Boy, was I tired that weekend! My granddaughter Sarah was with me all weekend so that did help me a lot. At least I had got more room with all those trays of preserves gone. However, I had still got eight full boxes put to one side for the Christmas Fair.

At weekends I used to write my column (and still do) for the East Anglian Daily Times and I also used to do my bit on Radio Suffolk. Mark Murphy used to come out mid-week and do a recording with me on gardening jobs to be getting on with and also about what was on in the area. My mind was always full, no wonder I had headaches. I remember one day in October we were having a '*Right Suffolk Night*' at Framlingham with Radio Suffolk. That morning I woke up with a splitting headache. I had to sit and have a rest for most of the day. By the evening I felt better and we had a good show with all local characters doing a turn. My late mother and sisters would all suffer with bad headaches so I suppose it runs in the family. My son rang to say that contracts were ready to sign and that I should be able to move on 23rd October. I went to the Harvest Service at Charsfield and was given a nice leaving card. I still didn't know for sure if the 23rd was going to be the date as there was some hold up with the paperwork. In the meantime the lady buying my house asked if she could bring some of her bits and pieces and put them in my sheds. Also she wondered if she could put up a new summer house and lay some slabs. I agreed.

At last we had a set date - 25th October. Allan asked if we could put some of my house contents in the garage at the bungalow. We were told we could at our own risk. My brother, Russell and Allan got a van and took some of my things on the 21st. What a day! It just poured with rain and I felt so sorry for the men as they got soaked. There was a lot of flooding round the villages. On the 24th the lady who was buying my house came round, very upset, and said she had nobody to help her. She said that she felt like pulling out. I felt awful. "You are lucky," she said, "you have your brother and two sons." I just asked her not to pull out at such a late stage and offered to ask my brother if he would help her. I asked Ronnie and he agreed. She felt better but I don't think Ronnie was very pleased with me for telling her he would help. He was very cross that night and would not speak. You can guess that I did not sleep.

Akenfield in the early Years

Chapter 2

Leaving Old Friends

October the 25th was the day I left the village with so many memories from over 41 years. My daughter-in-law and granddaughter came over on the morning I moved and helped me to finish cleaning and hoovering up. As my last pieces of furniture - bed, etc., were loaded on the van I had a last look round and walked up the garden to say goodbye to the chickens. Then I got into my car with my granddaughter as the new owner was arriving and wished her all the best. I said goodbye to Ronnie and as I was only going to be seven miles away I told him I would soon be seeing him. However he was not very happy. My old neighbours, Pam and David, had invited us round for drinks a night or so beforehand so I had said goodbye to them. We had always been good neighbours to each other. A year or so later they moved to Wickham Market and so did Thelma and Henry, my other good friends from my little lane in Charsfield. It was strange that so many families were leaving the Lane and the village after so many years.

Back to my move. I felt very sad as I drove towards my new home. Then the car started to get hot so I pulled to one side at the bottom of 'Drag Arse Hill' in Wickham Market and found that the fan belt had broken.

I expect you will think that this is a strange name for a hill! The story we have been told was that in 1698, on 10 February, John Bullard senior and his son John Bullard junior, millers at Letheringham water mill, were both murdered by their servant, Jonas Snell, a journeyman working at the mill. Snell attempted to escape but was later caught and tried at the Wickham Market sessions where he was found guilty. His body was dragged on a hurdle and hanged in chains on the Potsford Gibbet in a nearby wood, an awful warning to passers-by on the road. So this is where we get the name 'Drag Arse' applied to the steep hill on the B1078. The bones remained hanging until 1740 and the ghost of Jonas was, and still is, reputed to haunt the lonely crossroads and even lonelier woods. The gibbet post still stands and was surrounded by iron railings by public demand. The footpath was re-opened in 1955. A mixture of oak, ash and beech trees were planted and the gibbet was scheduled as an ancient monument. Despite hurricane damage the post and path have survived.

My late husband Ernest did not like cycling along the Potsford Wood Road as he always said he saw a ghost one night coming home from Wickham Market. We laughed and pulled his leg but he was serious about it and believed it was true.

Sarah phoned her dad and he soon came over and got me driving the car again. We arrived at my new home but could not get the key until 3pm. There was a hold up with the agent or the solicitor, I can't remember which. Once we had the keys my sons and their families soon got my bits and pieces all moved in then we went round to my son Allan's home and Jackie gave us all a good meal. I don't know what I would have done without them. I came back, looked around and said to myself, "Now old gal, you have got to settle down and make yourself contented." I got to bed, tired and with my head aching.

Next day I was up early as I had been awake for some time. A workman came in to install extra telephone points. Allan and his family came to help me unpack; there were so many boxes to move around. As I couldn't have portable bookcases I thought I would have the small bedroom made into an office. So I arranged with my odd job man to put up some shelves on the walls. I have so many books, I have to put them somewhere and as I am on my own I only need one bedroom. I planned to make the other room into a dining room. The small room to be made into the office has a nice outlook onto my small garden with a bird table and feeder near my window. As I unpacked boxes the clocks went back one hour and I realised I would have to get used to the long, dark evenings once again. My odd job man came to put up the shelves. The grandchildren came round and helped me to empty boxes and took a lot away so I had more room. I must say it was nice to be on one level with no stairs to climb.

I had very good neighbours where I lived before and was very sorry to leave them. But I soon found I had more good neighbours in my new home. The gentleman from next door brought me a pot plant and a card of welcome the day after I moved in and other neighbours soon were ready to have a chat and hoped I would be happy in their little road. For the first few weeks I had to get used to the quietness. It's strange as you would think that it would be more noisy living in a built-up area after living in the country but for weeks I could not get used to not hearing the tractors and lorries going by. I must admit the B1078 where I lived before was a busy road. As days went by I began to get things straight and books were put up on my new shelves. Allan finished hanging my pictures and it began to look like home. I do thank God that I can drive as my doctor, who is in Wickham Market, had said I could continue to be a patient there, which I was very glad about as they have always looked after me well. So the next thing was to get my flu jab done for another year. I decided I would try it once again even though it has upset me before; I would have to wait and see.

I had to go back to Charsfield to a Parish Council meeting where I was given a Notcutts Voucher for serving as a Councillor and Chairman for a number of years. I would miss this work and the phone calls. For weeks it seemed strange not being asked to help with some organisation or other but with the way I had been feeling it was good to have a rest and put my legs up as they had been playing me up.

I had been thinking about a small conservatory leading from my back door. My sons thought it was a good idea as long as I didn't fill it up with preserves, they said! I also had a new front door put on and the builders started work on the conservatory in the first week of December.

I was still doing a slot on BBC Radio Suffolk and I had been asked if I could make a rabbit pie while Lesley Dolphin, the presenter, watched me and told the listeners how it was done. There had been a lot of talk about rabbit pie. Allan got me two rabbits, which I had to skin. I find this job more difficult with arthritis in my hands. I have known a time when I could skin half a dozen in no time at all.

To make the pie you will need one rabbit, skinned and cleaned, cut into joints. Wash and put into a saucepan with fl lb belly pork, one small onion cut up and cook with 1fi pints of stock using the joints with the most meat on. Sometimes I use two rabbits as I take the rib joints out because there is not much meat on them. Cook for about one hour until tender. Let this cool. Then put this into a pie dish and season with salt and pepper. Make up short crust pastry. I use 1lb S.R. flour, fi lb fat (half lard, half margarine) and water to mix. Roll out. First put the pie funnel in the centre of the dish of rabbit to hold the pastry up and to let the steam out (if you don't have a pie funnel use an egg cup). Lay the rolled out pastry over the dish. Decorate with a fork, brush over with beaten egg and cook in the centre of the oven for about fl hour. This has been a Suffolk dish for years and was traditionally eaten on Christmas morning for breakfast (my late father loved it). After my slot making rabbit pie, I had Mark David ring me up to ask if I would do some cooking for '*Suffolk Magazine*'. He wanted me to cook some old Suffolk recipes but more of that later.

I had builders and gardeners come to give estimates for putting gravel down in front of my bungalow as the grass was uneven and I thought it would be easier to keep tidy. When you move house, however much you throw out, you still find you have far too much so for weeks I was putting bits and pieces in boxes and taking them to charity shops. Then months later you are looking for the very things you have given away! I had also been getting ready for my new book to come out called '*Countryside Year*'. A friend's sister, who was at home on sick leave, went through all the columns that I had written since 1986 picking out the most interesting pages and recipes. This was a big job for her but she had been in publishing so she knew what to look for. She and I had a lot in common as I had had breast cancer in 1994 and now she had got it. I told her to be positive but as the book was finished she became very ill and died in the summer. I was so pleased that she had seen the book published as she told me it had helped her when she felt too unwell. I must say I was lucky; my cancer was caught in time where so many women have been unlucky. I was in the Ipswich Hospital in Heath Road and I could not have had better treatment. It was in February 1994. My friend Iris had been in hospital just four weeks previously for the same operation. As I got out of my bath one night I found a lump under my arm. I made an appointment to see my doctor, Dr. Cragg at Wickham Market. He was so kind and told me that he wanted me to go to the hospital the following week to see Mr Adair. Iris came with me. He was another very kind consultant and told me I would have to have an x-ray and then see him. I went to the department, undressed and lay on the bed. A nurse rubbed some jelly on my breast and with a machine my breast was shown on a screen. Another man came in the room and I heard him say to the nurse, "Oh dear". From that moment I knew something was wrong. I got dressed and the nurse gave me the x-ray photos to take back to Mr Adair. I sat in the waiting room with Iris and all sorts of things were going through my head. I was then called in to see Mr Adair. He said he was sorry they had found a lump which they believed to be cancer and he asked me if anyone was with me. He went on to say that they would have me in to perform an operation in seven days time. My mind was in a whirl. I got home and how I cooked my brother's tea I don't know. He asked me how I had got on and I told him that I had to go into hospital as I had breast cancer. We did not say much to one another. Ronnie had been a smoker but I must say he packed up right away. I think he was worried that the smoke would upset me but, as I had told him, we didn't know why the cancer had come. Some people say we all have it and it just depends on whether or not it grows. Somehow I don't think so; what will be, will be. However I had to get on and try to think positively. I had my operation for a full mastectomy. All went well and Mr Adair told me that he hoped they had got all the cancer cells. After a few days Mr Mott, the oncologist, came to see me. He put me at ease and pulled my leg about the articles I write for the East Anglian Daily Times each week.

"I always read them," he said.

He was such a cheerful man and we have remained friends ever since. I still visit him and his wife. They have a lovely old farmhouse and garden. He keeps Kune Kune pigs as pets and they sit and beg like a dog for titbits. He is a wonderful man who has so many friends who have had cancer. He made me feel at ease right from the start. However, after he left my bedside telling me I would have to come to hospital for radium treatment twice a week for three months I sat on my bed and started to cry. A nurse came along and pulled the curtains around the bed and held my hand. She told me not to worry. Then who should put his face around the curtain but the Rev. John Waller from Waldringfield. The nurse looked up and said, "Oh look, here is your husband come to cheer you up."

How John and I laughed. John has been a dear friend for years and still pulls my leg saying, "Husband calling" when he phones. His father, the Rev. Trevor Waller, married my parents.

I left the hospital after a lot of kindness and started my radiation treatment which finished after three months. I had to cancel a lot of talks but was able to do them at a later date. I had to look at things and think about things positively. You just have to get on with life, however I could not help thinking about my sister Eileen who died on July the 10th 2001. She was only 56. She had gallstones and had told my sister Pat that she had been feeling ill for a while but then she had to go into hospital for a tummy operation. I shall never forget the phone call I had the night after her operation when I was told they could not do much for her as she was full of cancer. We only had four weeks and three days with her from the time she had her operation. I felt numb.

Eileen was very brave. She never once mentioned that she had cancer after the operation. I used to try and talk to her, saying that she could try some treatment. However, she refused, saying that she wanted to go home, which she managed to do for a few days. Then she was moved to the St. Elizabeth Hospice.

Eileen was a hard-working girl. She was always helping people and did not like it when she had to stop work as a carer at Mills Meadow in Framlingham. She would always be collecting raffle prizes for various organizations to which she belonged. In her younger days she played football for a ladies team in Suffolk and was so pleased to get a photo of the team in the T.V. Times. Like me, Eileen collected press cuttings and kept a scrapbook on Framlingham. She followed Ipswich Town Football Club. After her death I gave all her scrapbooks to the Lanman Museum in Framlingham with the permission of her two sons Steven and Garry whom she idolised. She was always talking about them.

We loved our sister, as did many people, in spite of her being '*John Blunt*' and calling a spade a spade!

The Farming Press had asked me before my operation if I would like to make a video of my garden month by month. I think this kept me going. I did get tired at the time but with my brother's help we got it done. It gave me something to look forward to and I am so pleased I now have a record of the garden, as when we were making it I never thought I would be moving away seven years later.

I told Ronnie the Farming Press wanted to make a video of the garden. He soon said he would help me to do this. We did have some laughs as Ronnie can be very dry in his humour at times. Peter Melling was the camera man. He and Ronnie got on well and shared some jokes. The video started off with views of Easton where I was born, also showing the picturesque cottage at Kettleburgh where my late grandfather, John Balls, lived. He was a very good gardener and I have the trophies he won at flower shows.

Endless Toil at Harvest Time

I begin the video by setting up potatoes for planting, sowing seed and picking out seedlings. Ronnie is getting the seed bed ready, planting broad beans, carrots, beetroot, parsnips, onions and cutting cauliflowers. Views are seen of Hoo Church and the Flower Festival in Charsfield Church, judging at Ipswich Flower Show, tomatoes in the greenhouse and my grandchildren, Russell and Sarah, with their names on marrows. There are shots of blossom time, plus primroses and cowslips. We also see Ronnie harvesting onions and the rest of the vegetables. The video finishes with Charsfield school children bringing gifts for Harvest Festival and singing "We plough the fields and scatter".

Back to my move. For weeks I was moving things and trying to find new homes for all my belongings. We were getting close to the festive season and Mark David called to pick me up to go and cook some recipes for the '*Suffolk*' magazine. Mark has a cookery studio at his home in Hadleigh and teaches students and housewives (and househusbands) how to cook. I enjoyed my day as I had to make Suffolk rusks (the times I am asked how to make Suffolk rusks!). They are so plain and so cheap to make but so popular! We then made a rabbit pie, a Felixstowe tart and talked in general about traditional country recipes. I had a lovely day with Mark and the photographer. I came home feeling rather tired.

People are always asking me for the recipe for Suffolk rusks. They are so easy to make. They are not a rich cake and they are what farm workers would have in their lunch bags. These were also taken to the fields at harvest time. They are like a scone to make but it's putting them back in the oven to dry them off that makes the rusk. My recipe is as follows:

1lb S. R. flour
Good pinch of salt
6oz fat (3oz lard, 3oz margarine)
2 eggs
A little milk or water to mix

Method: rub the fats and salt into the flour, then with the beaten eggs mix to a smooth dough. Roll out to one inch thickness and cut into rounds (2½ inches) and bake at 450 F for about 10 to 12 minutes. Remove from the oven and open with a fork, then return to the oven for a further 10 minutes or until they are a nice golden brown. When cold these rusks are delicious with a bit of butter or cheese.

(Note: some people use only one egg but if I have two I use them. It helps to make a nicer rusk).

Chapter 3

Settling In

I had been at my new home for two months and still couldn't get used to the quietness. There are over seventy houses in this little estate but it's oh so quiet. Thank goodness I had my writing to do for my column each week. I love writing this but I like to do it three weeks ahead so sometimes my weather sayings are wrong with the change of climate. I have been writing this column for 21 years now and have made and met so many friends through the newspaper. Sometimes I sit and wonder what I am going to write about this week but something always comes up. My son Allan is a country boy at heart and he often comes in and tells me he has seen this or that. "That's something you can write about, Mum," he says. So many people have sent me letters saying how much they enjoy the articles. Also it's nice to read about the past in the country instead of all the terrible things that are going on in the world today.

Before I knew it, it was my first December in my new home. I have always enjoyed helping to decorate the churches at Hoo and Charsfield but this year the weather took a turn for the worse making driving difficult. I did not feel very well and had to have some antibiotics for my chest. However, I met my brother, Ronnie, and he helped me do a window at Hoo Church. The roads were very icy so I didn't go to the service at Hoo. The vicar from Framlingham could not get to the church either for the Crib Service. By Christmas Eve the weather still hadn't cleared up so I wasn't able to make it to midnight mass. But would you believe it? The snow and ice had gone by Boxing Day. There were still sharp frosts; it had been the worst cold spell for a number of years.

The new year 2003 started with floods as there had been so much rain. I have always kept a diary so I have a good record of the weather. It's a good thing if you are a gardener to keep a diary. You would be surprised how things have changed over the years. I was still looking at my back garden to work out how I wanted the layout. In the meantime my publisher had asked me if I would like to do some scrap books on Weather Sayings and Suffolk Words and Sayings and also Cookery and Gardening Hints. So I set about writing sayings down. I also had a lady from the British Library in London ask me if I would do some tape recordings. She said she would come later in the month. Louise Brodie was here for two days; she stayed the night at Bredfield Bed and Breakfast. I felt so tired after two days of recording about my life but I suppose I should be grateful as not many people have their life recorded.

In the new year I was still busy doing my weekly slot on BBC Radio Suffolk, it was also early in the new year that I had my conservatory put on the side of the house so I could put my plants in for the winter. I still had too much furniture so I arranged for some to go in a sale. I had bookings to give talks as some bookings are made one year ahead. I was still giving talks but not driving as far as I used to. At one time I thought nothing of driving some 50 miles to give a talk but as you get older you don't want that long drive home. Ronnie came over and helped me to lay out the back garden. There was a big rockery in the corner. We took it all down as I thought I would get a small greenhouse. At the Benefice Supper in February back in Charsfield I was presented with a cheque and two rose bushes. It was such a surprise. So I bought my greenhouse with some of the money from the villagers' gift.

Memories were brought back to me as I heard on the radio that Princess Margaret had died on the 9th February 2002. I thought about when she visited my old garden at Charsfield, I had also met her at the Woman of the Year event and at the Suffolk Show. She had told me that she loved the film '*Akenfield*.' When the Princess visited, she stayed for 1½ hours and, after exploring the garden, she sat in my little sitting room looking at Akenfield photos. After her visit, Rex Pyke,

I missed the Owl calling
photograph - Clive Martin

producer of the film, made her a special video of Akenfield. After this I used to watch with interest Princess Margaret's visits and public appearances. After she died I told my son that I would love to have a catalogue of her items in the sale Christies were handling. Allan looked on the internet and said, "Mother, the catalogues are £75 each and you can't buy one!" I sat and thought about it and decided I would write to the director of Christies, telling him about Princess Margaret's visit to my garden and sending a paper cutting with the letter. Within two days his secretary rang me and said they were putting a catalogue in the post but it was very heavy and you couldn't lift it with one hand. I was so pleased to receive a copy within a week of writing. My son was surprised when I showed him the catalogue.

In February the decorator came in and did some odd jobs. One never seems to have enough electricity points so I had more put in. My daughter-in-law, Jackie, is a WI member but sadly Melton WI packed up so she joined Hasketon and asked me if I would like to go with her as I had been a WI member for years. In fact I got the WI in my old village, Charsfield and Dallinghoo WI, going. You are never too old to learn and you hear interesting talks. Jackie is very clever with her lace and patchwork quilt making. For my birthday in my first year at Riverview she made me a wonderful quilt for my double bed. The patterns include: Suffolk Puffs, Grandmother's Flower Garden, Corner to Corner curves - forming the River Deben, migrating geese and lastly there are skinny triangles representing the bungalow roofs in Riverview. This was the nicest present I could have had. Allan and Jackie put my greenhouse up so I was soon sowing a few seeds and taking cuttings, etc. I also went to see my old friend David Howard at Wortham who gave me some nice perennials. He has a wonderful wholesale nursery with so many varieties of plants. It was sad that the Queen Mother died on March 30th that spring of 2002. She loved her garden.

Friends John and Daphne have a pony so each time

they came to see me they would ask if a wanted a couple of bags of muck for my garden. I would always accept their offer, as the soil was like cinder dirt. The lady next door would come round and have a cup of coffee. She was so interesting to talk to and she would tell me stories from her life.

In May I was asked if I would open the new market which was going to be moved from the Hill in Woodbridge to the Budgen Car Park on Thursdays, still in the town. I am not sure why they wanted to move it but it's a small market consisting of a big fruit and vegetable stall plus a few other stalls. As you can see I still get asked to do talks as well as open events. The other one I did in May of that year, at the request of the Friends of Ipswich Christchurch Park, was rather unusual. It was to open '*Park Mobile*' rides. These were to operate in the park and could be hired by groups only. I had a nice day as I was taken for a ride round the park and I could see it would be a treat for people who can't walk far. I was given a super bouquet of flowers for cutting the ribbon. I don't think there are many people in East Anglia who have had the pleasure of opening the variety of events I have, from opening fêtes, old people's homes, planting trees and so on. I was still going back to church at Hoo and helping with the annual barbecue but was finding that I was getting much more tired. Perry and Margaret, my friends at Hoo, do a wonderful job but they are no spring chickens either! The local barbecue is a very popular event but I don't think people realise what a lot of work goes into organising it. Hoo holds theirs in a local farmer's barn so all the chairs and tables have to be collected from a local village hall, then plates, dishes and cutlery have to be borrowed before you even start to get all the food together and prepare it all to make funds for the local church. Then there is the raffle, selling tickets and asking people to donate prizes. It's not an easy task and you will notice in most villages that it's always the same people doing the work.

The summer months arrived and I still enjoyed doing

some judging at local shows. I have noticed that some shows had deteriorated in the last few years. Many of the old showmen have passed on and the younger generation do not seem to want to show. We used to have a very good show at Ipswich. I was their President for a number of years. Sadly we had folded earlier in the year due to lack of support. I still enjoy going to the Thompson and Morgan press day each year and meeting up with other garden journalists.

As I have said, I am asked to judge at many shows. I belong to the Suffolk Horticultural and Produce Association, which is an organisation that helps villages with their flower shows and insurance. There is a full committee and at one time there were over 70 clubs affiliated. We always used to have inter-village shows with a shield and cups for the winners.

Judging is based on the RHS Handbook. We are always on the look-out for new judges and if anyone is interested they can go round with a judge to learn the basics. Some thirty years ago, I started as a student with the late Mr Harry Borham who took me on. He was very thorough, a great gardener and a showman, winning many prizes. He told me what to look for in vegetables and flowers. Tomatoes should always have their calyces left on and this applies to strawberries and raspberries too. Once you have taken up the potatoes, keep them covered or they will turn green in colour. Onions should not have too much skin taken off when showing. Condition and uniformity are the key to showing. Also the RHS Handbook is a must for all judges.

In August of the year 2002 I shall always remember hearing that two little girls were missing form Soham, near Cambridge. As a mother and grandmother I really felt for the families involved. I have a friend, Marie Laffin, whom I met when I opened the Lakenheath Home a long time ago. It was awful when she told me that the girls had been found down a lane not far from her home. The whole country was outraged by this crime and it turned out that the caretaker from the school had killed them. Poor little dears, I expect they trusted him. People came from miles around to bring flowers to place in the local churchyard. It was like the flowers given for Princess Diana when she died.

Lakenheath is another village with which I have strong connections. In October 1983 the Lakenheath Vicarage went up for sale. A Lakenheath retired farmer bought it and decided to turn it into a home for the elderly. When local people needed care, many ended up miles away with friends and relatives not able to visit. With the help and advice from the late John Knights, a friend and solicitor from Bury St. Edmunds, a charitable trust was formed with six trustees to oversee the running of the home. It was called The Christian Enterprise Foundation.

This was opened on October 18, 1985 with six residents and eight more soon followed when an extension was built to take 14 residents. I carried out the official opening with the late John Knights in March 1986. It soon became obvious that more rooms were needed so a second extension was built with a further seven rooms, making a total of 21 residents. I again had the pleasure of opening the new extension with John Knights in August 1988. Mrs Angela Cook, SRN, was the first Matron. Her husband did the clerical work. They lived in a flat above the rooms. All the original carers were local girls and the friends of the home raised funds for residents. There was also a trolley shop once a week.

I have been over to see the residents at various times. They are happy and well cared for. This is how I got to know Marie Laffin, a former trustee, and a good friend over the years.

Chapter 4

Time for Hobbies

I have been writing about my books but my other hobby has been collecting postcards, mostly 80-100 years old, of Suffolk churches and villages. When I lived in Charsfield I never had the time to carry on this hobby as I would have liked. So now I found I had the time and started to go to sales, postcard fairs and second hand book sales. I remember my sons asking what I was going to do with my spare time after the move. I replied that I was going to try and collect postcards and photographs of all Suffolk villages and Suffolk churches. "Well you can sit and sort them all out!" was the boys' reply. I must say it is a very interesting hobby and is the third most popular 'collecting' hobby in the country (I'm sorry, I don't know what the first and second are!).

You would be surprised at the number of different postcard subjects there are to collect, such as dogs, cats, sports, anybody in uniform, railways, post offices, comic cards, in fact there are too many to mention. There are big postcard fairs held all over the country, with over fifty dealers sometimes. Woodbridge has now started with only about eight stalls. Over the past few years the price of cards has gone up. I used to pay about £2 per card (that is if they were 80 to 90 years old). Now they are £5 or more. Post office and railway station cards can fetch up to £25 each. The nearest postcard club to this area is Bury St. Edmunds. They also have a fair once a year with about 30 stalls. I take the Postcard Monthly magazine so that keeps me informed about postcards. I do like the old postcards as they tell of the changes over the years. Some people collect modern cards - these will be history one day.

You can also have cards on approval. Dealers will send them, you pick the ones you want then send the money and return the ones you don't want. Over the last few years ebay has had postcards up for auction and they sometimes sell at a high price. One from the Titanic made £500. Silk cards also make a lot of money. I tried to buy one on the Suffolk Regiment (which my father was in during the First World War) but the dealer wanted £50 for it. However, I have bought a lot of my collection at auctions but sometimes you have to buy mixed lots. Now I am choosy and only want Suffolk cards. People have told me you can buy Suffolk cards cheaper in towns further away from this area. I can see this makes sense. Years ago if you went on holiday you always sent postcards. Nowadays it's all texts on mobile phones or e-mails. What a new world we live in.

It was also the year when my eldest grandson, Russell, went to the Southampton Solent University. He gave me his old computer. I remember laughing and telling him I wouldn't be able to use it as I didn't even know how to turn it on! Sarah, his sister, said, "You'll learn, Grandma."
However, it sat in my little office for six months. Then I saw a notice about free lessons. I had met a lady from round the corner at a coffee morning and we had got talking and she said she would go to the lessons. One week I would take her and the following week she would take me in her car. Olive was very knowledgeable and used to type, so she could use her fingers quickly. I am a one finger typist and I still can't use the computer too well but I can send emails and I can look things up. I have seen postcards and books, then asked my son to get them as I don't like buying from the internet. If anybody had told me a few years ago that I would be using a computer I would have laughed at them. The one big regret I have is that I am not the world's best speller and would be lost without my dictionary.

As I have said, the computer is not my favourite piece of equipment. I suppose it's because I have not been brought up with one, like the school children are today. The times I hear my younger grandchildren saying they have been in their bedrooms working on the computer doing their homework! I must admit I am not the best scholar but I do get by. Perhaps

I should have paid more attention to my English teacher. I always laugh with friends and tell them I went to 'high school' (it was Kettleburgh School which is on a hill!).

I enjoyed going to my weekly computer class with Olive. She runs rings round me and is over 80 years old. She told me she could type and that helped her. I am still using one finger to type when I am trying to look things up . I do get in a muddle at times but I keep trying.

One thing I have learnt is that when you are looking up various subjects it's like looking at a book. My grandchildren have helped me a lot.

"Grandma, just put in www.google.co.uk and the subject you want and it will find it for you" they tell me.

Sometimes I can't believe that a small box-like thing can find you anything you want to know. But I still haven't got round to buying from ebay yet. Just looking will do me.

As I have said, my real love is books. I belong to the Adrian Bell Society. He was a country lover and I have a collection of all his books, as well as George Ewart Evans, H W Freeman and Allan Jobson, a well-known writer late of Felixstowe. These authors all loved the countryside. I am interested in any books to do with the history of Suffolk. My first book on Suffolk history I got at a jumble sale many years ago. It was called History of Suffolk by W White 1884. That started me off. My youngest son, David, brought me for Christmas one year the Suffolk Dialect by A D Claxton. I have found this so useful over the years. The Vocabulary of East Anglia 1830 is another good book. My other favourite which I use a lot is the two volumes of East Suffolk Illustrated and West Suffolk Illustrated by H R Barker, 1907-9. The illustrations are good and all the Suffolk churches are shown and many of the large houses that have now disappeared. I also had all the East Anglian magazines bound into 41 volumes from 1935 - 1982. My oldest book is by Robert Loder dating from 1798, I must not forget other favourite authors like Ronald Blythe, W G Arnott, R Simper, R Malster,

Norman Scarfe, Carol Twinch, David Kindred, and I could go on. So many books that give me so much pleasure, especially as I now have more time to read.

I missed many of the committees on which I had served but once I moved I thought that I would have a good rest. I did join the Monewden History Society which I enjoy. For a small village they have some good and knowledgeable speakers. For years I have been a member of the Suffolk History Society and look forward to receiving their notes twice a year. One way or another I do get plenty of reading matter.

As I have said, I have always been interested in history and do feel that Suffolk must be the most interesting county in Britain when you think about how much history we have and what has been found here. Perhaps some people will disagree but that is my view.

I look forward to a large packet each year from the Suffolk Local History Council with details of events, Society days and history weekends. We also get the Suffolk Review which is a booklet giving contents of manors, information on the fishing towns, local novelists and so on. There is a newsletter with details of recent books that have been published. It is very good to see what villages or towns are doing and their lists of speakers' names, well known people such as Dr John Blatchly, Clive Paine, Bob Malster, Pip Wright, Stuart Bowell, Roy Tricker, Sheila Hardy, Ivan Cutting, Peter Driver and many more. Forgive me for not mentioning you all.

Some of the most interesting history booklets were edited by the late Gwen Dyke and were called 'Deben Valley Place Names'. She visited and wrote about all our villages in the Deben Valley. Sadly she died while carrying out this work. I have twenty-two of these books. They give details of field names, the names of tithe maps, information on several agricultural revolutions, the two world wars, aerodromes and army camps, by-passes and dual carriageways, power lines, gas pipelines - I could go on. Village people got together and gave Gwen what they knew about their village. Gwen then put this information together. We owe so much to her for recording our local history and each year the History Society in Wickham Market (where she lived) holds a talk and supper called the Gwen Dyke evening which is always a sell-out.

Wickham Market has a strong history group and an Archive Centre in which Mary Morris and the committee run exhibitions at Easter and over the August bank holidays. Photos are displayed in the village hall. These are always very good. The Archive Centre is open to the public on Thursdays 10.30 - 12.30 p.m. in the hut at the back of the Village Hall. You can see documents and photographs, etc. More and more villages are now having their own history groups. It is so important to collect old documents or to ask the older generation about events that happened in your village. Once these people have passed on you have lost part of the history so put it down on paper or record them. If you have photographs try to put dates on the back (in pencil so they don't damage the photograph). I am the worst person to give this advice as for years I have taken photos and have forgotten to date them!

As my first year in Melton came to an end I had noted that it had been the wettest year on record. I had been back to the hospital and had had my tests done for my left knee replacement. We had snow and the roads were icy. This was rather unusual as our winters have not been bad in past years. I got to know my neighbours. A very nice bachelor lives on my left and we used to chat when I saw him in the garden. Joyce, the lady on the right, was having a lot of trouble with her legs and could not walk far. The nurse was coming in to do her dressings. She had relations who helped her and I used to do a bit of shopping for her.

At last, I had my date from the hospital for my long awaited knee operation; it was to be in February. Luckily there was a bed. This time I had an epidural anaesthetic in my back like a lumbar puncture which, for me, was so much better. I could hear doctors and nurses talking while the operation was taking place. I had a cup of tea as soon as it was over and there was no sickness. My stay was only nine days. I had got on very well; I had been in for nine weeks when I had had the right knee re-done, as it was wrong when it had been replaced two years before. I have a lot to thank the consultant Clare Marx for. She is a friend and a very clever lady. She goes all over the world teaching orthopaedic work. I owe so much to her. Once I got home I started to do my exercises and a little walk each day. After six weeks I was driving my car once again.

I have made many friends being on radio and writing my column in the East Anglian Daily Times. Many people know that I did a lot of charity work and this still leads many interesting and kind people to contact me. I remember one day when I was living at Akenfield I had a phone call from someone in Essex who wished me to go and see them as they had got something for me. It was in the middle of summer and I was pushed for time. I had a lot of people visiting the garden so I didn't like being away for long. On one particular day, however, I left Charsfield early and found the address of the place I was to visit. They were a nice couple and they made me very welcome. The gentleman told me he would like to give me something for the charities I supported. I thanked him and he said that he did not wish to be named as donor of this gift to charity. I told them both that I wouldn't do this but said that if I gave their gift to a charity I thought they should be thanked.

"OK," he said, "but no publicity."

I left their house, thinking that I must get back as I had a bus load of visitors to the garden arriving from London between 3 and 4 p.m. I got back, just put the carrier bag in the front room and got ready to meet the coach party. After the visitors had left at about 5 p.m. I put the kettle on and thought I would look at the carrier bag. I could not believe it, there was £6000 inside. Never had I handled so much money and to think I had just thrown the bag on my couch and forgotten about it for a while! Once I had come to my senses I rang my eldest son and told him the news.

"What do I do?" I asked.

"Well," he said, "the man must have given it to you in good faith. Have you got his phone number? Ring him!"

So this is what I did. He said I could use the money as I wished for my charities. I was gob-smacked. I gave the money to the St Elizabeth hospice and to the orthopaedic wing at Ipswich Hospital. But it did not stop there. I used to get phone calls from the nice couple saying they had more for the charities. I would then drive over to Essex to collect their donations and give it to Ipswich Hospital and the St Elizabeth Hospice. This went on until the dear old gent died. He used to love to talk about country ways and gardening. I shall always be grateful to him and his wife for their kindness. It always gave me a thrill to hand over the money and to know it was helping someone. Over the years I think I had about £11,000 of donations from them for the charities I supported. They did not wish their identity to be revealed but I told them they must be thanked. So I explained to the recipients that they must write to the couple and promise that their names would not be revealed as they wanted no publicity at all.

The year passed. I was still getting used to my smaller house but did enjoy everything I needed all being on one floor. I would sit in my little office with my books around me, looking out of the window to see the birds coming to feed. I had the radio on one day and pricked up my ears when I heard the announcement that Dame Thora Hird had died (15 March 2003). I remembered that it had been ten years since she had come to my garden at Charsfield. It was to do with her programme called ‘*Praise Be*’. She was so kind and friendly. My friend Perry had made a sponge cake and iced it with ‘*Praise Be*’.

When she saw it she said, "Oh, my Scotty (her husband) would love this."

So I gave it to her to take home. When she got back to London at 11 p.m. she wrote me a letter thanking me for a nice day. I thought she was marvellous as she could have got her secretary to write the next day for her.

I could not believe it when I heard that Dame Thora, as I used to call her, was coming to visit my garden. Thora was born in Morecambe, Lancashire on May 28, 1911. She married James Scott ('Scotty') in 1937. They had one daughter, Janette. Thora followed her parents into the theatre. I love her films. She also played a range of classical and contemporary roles on the stage and television starring in several comedy series. So many people used to write to her when she presented the popular '*Songs of Praise*' programme on Sunday evenings. Then we would watch her in the '*Last of the Summer Wine*' TV series. I can see her now putting down her newspaper when her husband came into the house. She played this part so well. How we used to laugh.

She was in over 50 films, over 20 plays on stage, the television specials, '*Meet the Wife*' and '*In Loving Memory*' and the one I loved was Talking Heads in 1988, '*A Cream Cracker under the Settee*'.

Yes, Dame Thora Hird was one of Britain's finest character actresses. She wrote her autobiography called '*Scene and Hird*' in 1976.

I feel very honoured to have met her. Another date which I put down in my diary was 20 March when we went to war with Iraq. Oh dear, I thought, our poor boys and girls off fighting again. Why do we have to have wars? There are no winners.

Many friends were coming to see me and my new home. One friend called Ruth came round and brought me a small bunch of spring shrubs and flowers. One of them called Daphne odorata variegata. It has small pink flowers and evergreen leaves. I put some cuttings in pots and I am so pleased as I have a fine shrub now; it is some 4 feet tall. As a rule it is rather difficult to take cuttings from this and get them to strike. On the subject of the garden, I had an odd job man come round and put some trellis up on my wooden fence around the garden as I thought this would be a good way of growing climbing plants. It is surprising how this makes the garden look bigger.

March and April were very dry and also much warmer than usual. Many local commons had been on fire, Hollesley was one of them. A visitor from Anglia Television came to see me in April as he wanted to do a write up in a magazine; many people will know Paul Barnes. Akenfield was having a reunion in November 2004 after 30 years- more about this later.

A friend rang me in early May to see if I would like to go and hear the nightingales in their small wood at Hasketon. I must say it was a wonderful sound. There may have been some thirty odd birds singing away in the night. I was able to talk about this on my radio slot as I was still making notes on the countryside and talking about these as well as giving gardening hints. In between I was making preserves; friends still used to bring me vegetables and fruit and I just couldn't let them go to waste. But my hands were becoming painful at times from cutting up vegetables, etc. As the summer months came I was often asked to do judging, which I still enjoy. One invitation was to judge Charsfield School paintings for their open day.

When I had moved from the village in October 2001 I had left charity money from the garden funds to be given to the Over 60's Christmas Meal. This event had been going on for many years. A group of us used to raise money to put on the meal. Then the church clock needed to be re-painted. We knew this was a specialist job and there is never money to spare for all the work needed on these fine buildings. So when I closed the garden I discussed this with my brother Ronnie. He said that the villagers like to see the time as they come down the hill into the village. As he had helped me so much in the garden we gave the church £1000. He rang me in July to say the scaffolds were up and the painting would soon start. The clock had a fading gilt paint on it. So I looked forward to seeing the end result but, oh dear, once it was finished you could not see the time unless you were near the church. I told the church council I was not happy and the builders came once more and re-did it. But it's still no better even five years later. I look at the clock and wish a specialist had painted it and had not used the brown paint. It's done now but I still feel disappointed when I visit the village.

Alan James, who makes videos, asked me if he could make one on my life as I still had a lot of tapes left over from the Farming Press which Peter Melling took when he worked there. Alan asked me where I would like to finish talking about my life, in some garden or nice setting. I would have liked to have gone to Beth Chatto's garden but the weather was very warm and I did not feel too well. I thought about Helmingham gardens so we wrote to Lady Tollemache and she said yes. So we met in July. Lesley Dolphin, the BBC Radio Suffolk presenter, was my interviewer. We were working until a quarter to seven, finishing up in my garden. I was so tired and hot, it had been a busy day. I was glad that I could rest the next day. We were not used to this heat wave which had hit our small country so early in the summer.

I was pleased with the video. Second Sight Productions put it together well, using some of my family photos. I was proud to think mine was the first council house listed in the Yellow Garden Book, along with the big estates. The video shows me making wine, marmalade and lemonade. Also I tell of the hard times my mum and dad had working on the land. My father had Parkinson's disease early in life so times were difficult, with five children to bring up. My husband left the land in the 1950's. We were in a tied house which meant the house went with the job. If you left your job you had to find another house. So this is when we got a council house in Charsfield in 1960.

The video shows how I use the fruits of the earth for preserving. It also shows my many visitors to the garden, including royalty and the Gardeners' World team. It shows the Rev. John Waller taking Ronnie and me on his boat '*Jesus*' on the River Deben to go and pick samphire to pickle. My aim has always been to show how you can use vegetables and fruits, etc. I also tell how we made the film '*Akenfield*' and show different scenes. I talk about my visit to the USA and my trip on the QE2. The video covers my life very well.

Thora Hird at Charsfield

Chapter 5

Looking Back

I still couldn't get used to having more spare time and even being able to go out more. My cousin John and his wife Audrey asked me if I would like to go to see East Bergholt church and its outside bell cage. They knew I liked to visit churches so this was a nice outing. There had been many times when I would have liked to have gone sightseeing in the past but I did not like to leave the garden back at Charsfield. I bet the church at East Bergholt gets many visitors as it is in Constable Country. It's worth a visit as this beautiful and interesting church is the village where the famous artist was born. There is a unique bell cage which stands outside, next to the church. It sits attractively under a tiled pyramid roof. The bells in their frame can be seen through the lattice of the timbered walls. The bell ringers do not use ropes; they stand on the frame and control the bells with wooden stays. There is so much history to this church. There is one brass on the floor. It commemorates Robert Alfounder. He was once a church warden, dying in 1639.

I was also interested in the large building opposite the church which I was told used to be a Benedictine Convent. At one time there were 60 nuns, 4-5 sisters and a priest there. In 1940 when the Second World War was on, it was feared that the Germans would invade. I was reading from the Suffolk Women's Institutes that one morning all the inhabitants of the convent had packed up and left. The convent was later requisitioned by the Army with the officers' mess in the little courtyard. I am not sure who has the old convent now but there is a lot of old history about this village. With all of my days out and new visitors I felt like I had a new life. At the same time as visiting East Bergholt, I went to the fête at Hasketon, the church had so many nativity sets on display. It was unusual to see them in August but I did enjoy looking at them. After looking round the fête I walked over to the church, St Andrew's, with its round tower. I understand it was remodelled around 1300 when a window was inserted and an octagonal bell stage added, making it the tallest round tower in Suffolk after Mutford church. I do love round towers so it is good to see this one so near to my home, sheltered by beech trees with its octagonal top looking across farm lands.

St Andrew's is very old. It is possible that it was built as early as the 14th century by Richard de Brewse. The long, narrow windows could have been arrow slits. On walking round the church, you find the east wall of the chancel was re-built, a vestry added and the porch renewed in 1850. Most churches now have fine embroidery hassocks. It's worth looking for them in the church you are visiting, they have some superb designs. The best place to see the villages represented is at Bury St. Edmund's cathedral where hassocks from all the villages and towns are all in rows in the pews. It's a wonderful sight. The weather was still very hot and there were still many fires on commons. The firemen had a busy time; this must have gone on record as the hottest, driest year. I went to Walsham le Willows to do some judging. Driving there I thought how dry the countryside looked.

In August of that year John, Audrey and I visited one of the best wholesale nurseries in the country. I got to know David Howard when I was with Radio Orwell. He grows hardy perennials and helps many people with displays at the Chelsea Flower Show. His nursery is at Wortham, near Diss in Norfolk. He and his staff are so kind and friendly. John used to work in a nursery and park in Ipswich so I wanted to show him David's large set up. That very year, 2003, eleven medal winning gardens had had plants from Howard Perennials. He even supplied the Best Show Garden with his plants. We enjoyed our day and David gave me a box of plants for my new garden.

I was still giving many talks; in August I went to give one in Mildenhall. I felt so tired when I got home, my legs were playing up and I thought I would have to cut down on all this driving. My next talk in September was in Shimpling. Friends came to the rescue and drove me there to show slides on the garden. It was a nice evening and so good of the friends to take me.

In October my neighbour Joyce's house was being cleared. Her relatives gave me bits and pieces, which I passed on to friends who were running a sale for the St. Elizabeth Hospice. The St. Elizabeth Hospice has always been a charitable organisation that is close to my heart. The foundation stone of the hospice was laid on July 8th 1988 by the Duchess of Norfolk after years of campaigns and publicity to get a hospice in Suffolk. I first learned about this years before when I met Robert and Phyllis Marjoram (known as Bob and Phil to many) who were regular visitors to Akenfield. They spent much of their time touring local villages giving talks and showing slides about how they were hoping to build a hospice. As I was giving talks on Akenfield at this time we used to meet and discuss the villages we had visited and share recommendations. Bob did so much in making the public aware of the need for a local hospice and his wife helped raise funds through her stall in Ipswich hospital selling jams and pickles etc. I helped the fund by donating money raised through my garden, and continued to give a share of the proceeds to the hospice from then on. One day when donating money to the hospice from my garden proceeds I was lucky enough to be joined by Sir Bobby Robson, we had a photo taken together. Years later in 2007 when he won the BBC Sports Personality of the Year Lifetime Achievement Award I wrote to him asking if he remembered that day and telling him about the hospice today. He wrote a lovely reply detailing his memories and saying how he was always sure the hospice would do well.

In 1975 the National Society for Cancer relief (Macmillan Fund) gave East Anglia a sum of money to build a hospice. My friend Terry Mott, consultant in oncology at Ipswich hospital represented Ipswich at a meeting of the regional health authority, but the money was given to Norwich, this became Priscilla Bacon Lodge. More money was then allocated to Cambridge which became Arthur Rank House. After this no more money was available for hospices, so Ipswich had to find its own money.

In 1980 an appeal for a CT scanner for Ipswich hospital was launched, this was chaired by Tom Savage, secretary of the Felixstowe Dock Company, this was a great success and the scanner opened in 1982. Terry Mott drafted in Tom's support to chair and launch a hospice appeal. A competition for the name of the new hospice was launched in the East Anglian Daily Times, with a prize of a television set for the winner! There was one entry for 'Saint Elizabeth' which won. Saint Elizabeth was a compassionate Christian who built a hospital and cared for its patients. She is also the reason behind the rose emblem of the hospice, legend has it that one day she was delivering loaves of bread to the poor, a practice unpopular with the aristocratic men she bumped into on her way to the poor cottages. These men stopped and asked what she was carrying, she answered "roses". Elizabeth knew that she had told a lie, and stood blushing, however when the man pulled aside her cloak to see what she was carrying, God intervened, so legend has it, and turned the loaves into red and white roses.

The fund raising began in earnest, with most of the money coming from small donations and local events. The hospice opened its doors in 1989 and was formally opened by Princess Anne a little later. Today the hospice continues in its role of giving expert and compassionate care to the people of East Suffolk. It receives just over one third of its running costs from the NHS and relies on the generosity of the public as well as its capable volunteers for the rest.

Joyce was now settled in a residential home in Woodbridge. I was still giving talks; 2003 was a busy year. I went to Somersham Garden Society, Grundisburgh and to Mr Hope Cobbold's home at Glemham for the Saxmundham

History Society. In November, Joyce's house was sold and I met my new neighbours, Frances and Vick, who had bought the house. I heard on the 8th November that Joyce had died. I went to her memorial service at Bredfield, remembering her with kindness. I would have loved to show her my video, which had come out in time for Christmas. On December the 14th, we heard that Saddam Hussein had been found alive in a hole in the ground in Iraq. On December the 17th the Soham murderer got two life sentences for killing the two little girls and his girlfriend got $3\frac{1}{2}$ years. Then on December the 26th, Iran was hit by an earthquake killing over 25,000 people. What a way to end 2003.

In the New Year Ivan Howlett, who used to be in charge of BBC Radio Suffolk, rang me. After he had retired, he used to do recordings for BBC Radio 4. He asked me if I would talk about seeing my first cars in the countryside and my first taxi ride. Ivan will often ring to ask if I will do some recording for him. In February half-term week, I had two of my youngest grandchildren to stay and I took them to Sutton Hoo. It was a real eye-opener to me as I had never been there before. It is always the same - you live near to places of interest but never find time to visit them. I am sure George and Harry enjoyed it as they asked me many questions about the treasure found in 1939 in the remains of the Saxon ship. We only saw the replicas as the best were in London at the British Museum. I often wonder if they told their schoolteachers about the outing!

In March, I lost my step brother-in-law, George Mead. He was a wonderful man; I was so fond of him. You would call him the salt of the earth. He had worked on the land all his life and would help anybody. He never had a bad word to say about anybody. He was the local chimney sweep and he had an old railway carriage in which he would give haircuts to men and boys. He also used to wind the church clock each Saturday, all in his spare time. After his wife died, he used to visit me often on Fridays for lunch. I would invite other old friends too - Clifford Arbon from Monewden and the Rev. Jim Laurie - as they lived on their own. Oh, the tales they would tell! I wish I had recorded them. They were happy lunch hours with a little drink to keep them going. Clifford Arbon was a countryman, full of knowledge about the countryside. He never had much of an education. In fact, he told me his school days were hard. Clifford never got on with his teacher at Monewden where he was born in 1908 but whenever you saw him he had a smile on his face. On the other hand he could soon get 'riled' (annoyed) if someone upset him. He was a very clever wheelwright. He made everything by hand. He never went far from his village. He loved playing steel quoits.

"I was in the team that won the Woodbridge Cup seven times," he told me, "we were called the Monewden Scarlet Runners."

The church was also his life - singing in the choir, helping out with the Village Hall. In fact, his life was the village. Whenever suppers were organised with entertainment, Clifford was there making people laugh and often playing his accordion and giving a tap-dance. When he came down to have lunch with me he would always have a yarn to tell me. He loved his garden so we had many talks about ways of planting seeds, etc. His workshop and smithy is still open on Bank Holidays. It is like stepping into a forgotten age. You will find this in the village of Monewden.

In April, a man came to do some video recording on sugar beet hoeing. I had told him that in my early-married life I had helped my late husband with this work until in later years when this job was no longer done as sugar beet was all precision drilled. In the 1950's and 1960's many farm workers would take this job as piecework. It was hard work but it meant you could earn some extra money! My back and knees still suffer from all this hard work.

In May, I was asked to open the Nedging May Day festival (like an open fête). I left late morning in the pouring rain, hoping it would ease up but it just fell down. I got there at 12 p.m. but left at 2 p.m. as the committee felt it was not going to hold up. I felt so sorry for them as so much hard work goes into organizing these village events.

My Front Garden in Melton

Chapter 6

Akenfield - The Anniversary

May brought a phone call from Rex Pyke, the producer of Akenfield. He wanted to go round the old places where we had filmed Akenfield in 1974. He arrived at my home at Melton to pick me up and we drove around the villages. It was strange going back to the old scenes. He wanted to see the Akenfield sign I had left at my house in Charsfield. A lump came to my throat as I stood in front of my old home. The sign had dropped in the grass. It was rather a sad day. Rex later asked me if I could get in touch with all who were in Akenfield to tell them we were having a reunion after thirty years. I was given a list of names and spent hours phoning people telling them we were going to have wine and nibbles and the film would be shown at Ipswich Film Theatre on November 21.

Stowmarket Museum had asked me to give a talk so I was able to mention the Akenfield showing. The museum opened on 10 July 1967. Lord Euston stood in a Suffolk wagon and declared open the Abbots Hall Museum of Rural Life in East Anglia. Abbots Hall is a house built in the 18th century of red brick. The museum started in a small way but now houses on its 70 acres a unique collection of farm implements and horse-drawn vehicles. The open-air section opened in 1971 and includes the magnificent Edgar's farmhouse (1340's), an 18th century smithy taken from Grundisburgh and the Alton water mill with its cart lodge and miller's house, dating from the same period. There is a wonderful collection of tools and household objects.

Many schools take the children to the museum for day visits. There is so much for them to see and learn. There is also a nice shop and restaurant and for the last two or three years there have been demonstrations of various crafts. They hold traditional music days with guests who sing, step dance, play the melodeon, concertina and accordion - they all give fine displays. There are film shows and talks that you can book with suppers. The museum is open daily and I can assure you that it is well worth a visit. Then some friends I had stayed with when I had gone to New Jersey in America rang me to say they were staying in a bed and breakfast in Swilland near Otley. They wondered if we could meet up. It was so nice to hear from them and I arranged to go and see them in late May. We had a lot to talk about. Joan Morrison had arranged many of my lectures around America and had made me so welcome in her home. I first met Joan Morrison in the late 1970's when she visited my garden at Charsfield. She had bought Ronald Blyth's book 'Akenfield' published in 1969. She loved the book then went to see the film. She was so impressed with the film that she decided to look me up.

That started a long friendship over the years. Joan and her husband Robert had been coming to East Anglia for a number of years as Robert is a Professor of Chemistry and was having his books published at the well-known printers, Clays of Bungay. So he was often working while Joan was looking round East Anglia, which they both love. For a number of years they rented a property in Wickham Market so Joan came to some of my talks. Soon she was asking me if I would go and stay with them in Morriston, New York and give some talks for her clubs. This I did four times.

Joan is a well-known author. Her first book, 'American Mosaic' is all about the American immigrant experience. Men and women told her their stories; the late Alistair Cooke and Lynn Redgrave are but two of the names. They all reveal the mingled joy and pain and the gamble of a new life in a new land. Joan compiled this book with Charlotte Fox Zabusky who directed an immigrant programme for a number of years. Both Joan and Charlotte have lectured all over the country to universities on oral history and immigration. Her other book, 'From Camelot to Kent State' is all about the sixties and was another great success. Joan is now in her eighties and still gives lectures. I know her family are very proud of her. Sadly, as I write this, Robert is in a nursing home as he is not well. When I talk to Joan on the phone she is still her cheerful self. It has been a privilege to have got to know such a wonderful couple. Without Akenfield I may never have met them.

In June the hot weather started again. Rex had arranged for Sir Peter Hall to meet some of the old Akenfield cast at Hoo church (I had to get used to calling Peter 'Sir' as he had received this title since the filming of Akenfield). It was good to meet up with many of the characters. However, the weather was so hot and I was glad to do my interview with Peter in the cool church. He wanted to ask us all what we had been doing during the last thirty years. Later I had them back for tea. On the following day we met more of the film crew and people who were in the film. They met at the Old School in Debach and the Old Rectory. We had a lot to talk about. The film assistant and cameraman were so surprised to see how the old school had been changed into a very nice home. The weather was still warm for the next few days. My friend Daphne brought me some elderflower heads so I made a gallon of wine, the first lot I had made since moving to Melton. Friends were still bringing me fruit and vegetables so I still got on with making preserves and chutneys. In July a friend asked me if I would like to go to the Peak District for the weekend. We left Ipswich early on the Saturday morning visiting Sheffield, then looking at the well dressing in Eyam, Derbyshire. Then we went on to Chatsworth House, the home of the Duke and Duchess of Devonshire. The house is one of the treasure houses of England. I never thought I would be visiting the Duchess's home. I remembered interviewing her at the Chelsea Flower Show; it was on a press day and a new rose had been named after her. It was a lovely weekend. The only thing I had a job to cope with were the high steps when getting in and out of the bus. As the bus driver told me, he could not have a box or steps to help in case anyone slipped - apparently it is to do with the Health and Safety regulations.

After that week I went judging at the Co-op Show in Ipswich, then on to open a church fête at Cretingham. July was a busy month. I gave a talk in Lakenheath and went to the Thompson and Morgan press day. As the month passed, I was glad of a rest as I was doing nearly as much rushing about as when I had lived in Charsfield.

On the August bank holiday I collected my brother Ronnie and his friend Bud and we went to visit Crowfield Flower Festival in their little church. Like many of our village churches it is well away from the village, beautifully placed, hidden among the trees. When you first see it the end of the church looks like a village hall. The chancel is like a timber-framed cottage. It is a small, charming church and another one I had always wanted to visit. Now I could cross it off my list.

September, I feel, is a nice month with so much produce about. It is a busy time for people who like to make preserves. I remember one morning the phone rang. It was my friend Ronald Blythe. "Peggy," he asked, "could you meet a man called Craig Taylor off the train at Woodbridge and take him round Charsfield?" Craig wanted to write a book, meet the people in the village, and ask about the changes since Ronald had written his book 'Akenfield' in 1969. I met this young Canadian man and told him all about the village, gave him names of people to talk to and introduced him to many people. He wanted to write a book like Ronald had done and I told him it would have to be good to match 'Akenfield' which had been published in 1969! As I told him, many universities still use this book for English studies.

A friend took me to give a talk in Spexhall, a small village the other side of Peasenhall. The Women's Institute were very hospitable and even gave me flowers when I had given my talk. As the Akenfield reunion was approaching, I started to get reporters and journalists coming round to ask me about Akenfield and the last thirty years.

In October I took Craig to the Charsfield Harvest

Supper so he could see what village life was like and to meet more people. My brother Ronnie and his friend Bud were there and I think Craig had a job to understand their Suffolk dialect. Bud, as we call him, is a dear old boy in his eighties. He cannot read or write but what he knows about village life is amazing. I used to invite him round for a meal and would often bake him a cake. He would come and see me most days when I was in Charsfield, asking if I had any letters to post. He liked company and a chat and had been very upset when I told him I was going to move.

I had an invitation to Charsfield and Dallinghoo W.I.'s twenty-first birthday. I was asked to help cut the cake as I had got the W.I. going again after it had disbanded in earlier years.

October 2004 was busy. I went to the small village of Beyton to give a talk at their harvest supper and once more I took Craig Taylor with me. Also in this month I had an invitation to go to the Ipswich Hospital as the Duke of Kent was going to open a new wing for the cancer department and I am one of their patrons. It was a lovely day and so much work and fund-raising had gone in to achieving this wing, which would help many Suffolk people. Craig came to lunch and thanked me for my trouble in ringing people and making arrangements for meetings.

The Cancer Campaign in Suffolk was launched in 1998 to establish a central point in Suffolk for cancer support. A major fundraising campaign commenced to improve the access to and the quality of cancer information and support for Suffolk people. The first major project was the £350,000 cancer Information Centre that was built next door to the Suffolk Oncology Unit in Ipswich. With more than one in three people contracting the disease at some time during their lives, it was felt this would be a solid foundation on which to build the fight against cancer in Suffolk.

The Information Centre was needed as early diagnosis can only come from knowing what to look for and from knowing what to do if one suspects that there may be a problem. This Centre houses all the latest audio and visual aids for advising and informing about cancer, including access to the internet. There are three private interview rooms that are available to doctors, nurses, specialists, oncologists and other professionals to talk to patients, families, friends and carers about any problems that may be associated with the disease.

Although it has been built for East Suffolk, the facility is intended to serve the whole of the county with information about the disease. Information about other cancer charities is also available, together with details of local and national self-help and support groups. The Centre is now called the John Le Vay Cancer Information Centre after his death in March 2008, aged 51.

The Centre has been far more successful than we could have ever imagined since John Le Vay had his original concept and celebrates its tenth anniversary in September this year (2008). I must say at this point that John was a man dedicated to his work with cancer patients and loved by so many. He looked after me. I had so much confidence in him - not only was he a doctor, he was a friend to all he treated. I used to sit in the waiting room and hear other patients talking about him - such kind words. "How lucky we are to have him," they would say.

The next aim of the Cancer Campaign in Suffolk is to provide an all-purpose mobile cancer information service to the people who cannot travel to Ipswich. I hope I live long enough to see this. If Sir Bobby Robson can raise money for his cancer department in Newcastle-upon-Tyne, we can do it in Suffolk I am sure.

In November I had a request from the BBC to go to Ipswich and make a recording of what I could remember about the Second World War. They were travelling all around the country making recordings. I told them what I recalled about a USA plane crash at Easton and about how the American soldiers were so kind to us children, giving us gum and oranges, etc.

I was only a young girl during the Second World War but I do remember the doodlebugs coming over and Mother making my brother and I get under the kitchen table when the raids were on. It was awful when you heard the doodlebugs coming. You could hear the noise of the engine, and then it stopped suddenly. You then knew it was coming down very quickly. I must say, we lived in Easton at the time so I do not think we suffered as much as the town people did. My Dad was in the Home Guard and was out two or three times a week. In the winter we were glad of his Home Guard coat to put over our bed to keep us warm. Whenever we went out we always had to carry our gas masks in little boxes slung round our necks.

I think the war brought us together more, as people from the local villages used to enquire if you were all right. A lot of fund-raising was done for the men and women in the war. Working class people mixed more with the upper classes and more hospitality was shown. We were so pleased to see the Americans; they were at Parham and Debach, which was near to us. When we saw the first black American we just stood and stared with wide eyes.

I well remember one morning the sky was full of aeroplanes. My father said he wondered how many poor boys would come home. Later in life I learnt they were going to Arnhem. It was also in November that I met Paul Heiney at the Suffolk Show ground to launch the Suffolk Horse stud at Hollesley Bay. A new museum was to be built to enable people to get to know all about the Suffolk Punch. Hollesley Bay is a prison and the government wanted to sell the Suffolk horses. This is why a group of people had wanted to save the biggest stud of Suffolk horses in the country.

One day I had a surprise call from Peter Tuddenham, the only well known actor in Akenfield and also, the narrator. We had a nice chat and he told me he was looking forward to meeting us in London on the 20th November as there was to be a showing of the film at the National Film Theatre with the press. Garrow Shand (who played my son Tom in the film) and his wife collected me at 3.30 p.m. to drive to London. The National Film Theatre is on the South Bank. We met many friends, the film crew and the press who asked us questions. Garrow gave Ronald a lift home; it was a very cold night with a sharp frost. I got back to Melton at 2.30 a.m. and just fell into bed, very tired. The next day we all met at the Ipswich Film Theatre to see the film again. It was so good to see the people I had contacted who had been in Akenfield. I felt rather sad that thirty people in the film had since passed on. The schoolchildren in the film had grown up and it was a job to recognise everyone. However, it was a nice reunion and I do not think we shall see another one.

The following week, after I had had a good rest, I went to a gardening quiz for Easton Church. This was a good occasion, held at Easton Farm Park. Over the years I have had some pleasant evenings at the Park. Old farm buildings have been changed into a large room, like a village hall with a kitchen nearby. Many people have hired this room for functions. Whenever I drive through Easton village, I think of my parents who started their married life at Pound Corner Cottages. Then they moved to what was known as the 'uplands'. I am indebted to Peter Farley of Easton who has told me so much about Easton and the Dukes of Hamilton who played such an important part in the shaping of the village.

Easton has one of the best undulating crinkle-crankle walls. The man who built the wall and mansion was Anthony Wingfield who was made a Baronet in 1607. Later the estate was taken over by the Duke of Hamilton. I remember my late aunt telling me she nursed the First World War soldiers when the mansion was turned into a hospital. In all there were twelve dukes. The last one, William 12th 1845-1895 inherited the Hamilton estate at the age of 28. The Duke married Lady Mary 1854-1934 and together they spent a great deal of time and money on Easton, including the buildings of Easton Farm Park, which is well known today. It has one of the most interesting old dairies in the country with its octagonal shape and tiled walls. You have the Hamilton rooms nearby where many people have enjoyed happy times such as wedding receptions, parties, etc.

Back to the Farm Park. It is a wonderful place for children and it gives them the opportunity to find out about the countryside at first hand. Easton remains the ideal place for learning for families and schools in a rural setting. Today the environment is an issue of great importance and the Easton Green Trail gives everyone access to many indigenous birds and plant species. You can also see longhorn cows, poultry, Suffolk Punch horses, Gloucester Old Spot pigs, goats, geese, etc. There is a farmer's market once a month, which you can walk round freely. The children can look at the farm park while their parents shop. When you look round Easton you see houses and buildings, all with their black and white beams, and realise what a picturesque and historical village it is.

The year 2004 ended with myself and old friends, Margaret Doe and Janet Martin, on the panel at Monewden History Society, giving our memories of Christmas in the past. We did enjoy ourselves and had some good laughs. Monewden people have always been so hospitable. Then we had the Over 60's Christmas Party. Over the years I have learnt that it is not just the meal that is good but it is meeting old friends. With some people it is the only time you meet from one year to the next and it is just nice to have a good old 'mardle'; as we say in Suffolk.

My word, how Christmas has changed. Nowadays you see the young housewives coming out of the supermarket with their trolleys so full of food as if there is going to be another war. I think back to how we had the Christmas bird down the garden being fattened up (we only had chicken at Christmas). We had roast potatoes, parsnips, Brussels sprouts, all from the garden. If we had peas they came out of a tin; there was no frozen stuff. In November we helped Mum to stir the Christmas pudding (she made two - one for Easter). She also made Christmas cake and she let us help to ice it, mainly with silver balls. It was all good, homemade food. There were rusks and sponge iced buns. I cannot remember bought cakes ever existing.

In the morning we would come downstairs to see the Christmas tree as it was not decorated until Christmas Eve. We had our stockings and maybe two or three large presents. One year I had a needlework box, a black doll and an annual. We had some games like Snakes and Ladders, Ludo and Tiddly Winks. We thought it was wonderful if Father had a game with us. Sometimes the carol singers would come round but we were too young to go with them. My father used to do gardening for a woman in Easton and she always gave us nice presents. In addition, Mrs Hill, who kept the Kettleburgh Chequers, sent us gifts. I suppose my father was a good customer as he used to meet his workmates there and also his father for their weekly pint of beer.

Weeks before Christmas the schoolteacher would teach us about the coming of the baby Jesus. We spent days practising for our nativity plays, then we had school parties and Sunday school parties. How we looked forward to the iced buns, jellies and blancmanges! At the end of the party we were given an orange or apple and a few sweets done up in a twist of pretty paper. Children would laugh at you if you gave them that sort of food today. I know we were more content in those days. Our parents must have had to work and save very hard to give us such a happy Christmas. I am sad to write that the year finished up with one of the worst natural disasters we have ever seen. In Sri Lanka a Tsunami swept the shores and the water killed thousands and thousands of people, many of whom had been there on holiday from other parts of the world. Even years later bodies have not been found.

Chapter 7

Ronnie's Move

Another new year. I do not look forward to January or February for health reasons as I always seem to get bronchitis and suffer with my chest. My arthritis seems to be getting so painful but then I look around and see people a lot worse off then me. I do not take any bookings to give talks in winter months, as I don't like to drive at night. My first talk of the year was at Framlingham to the Monday Club. In April, Liz, another friend, took me to Hoxne to the Adrian Bell Society. We meet in different parts of Suffolk each year and have interesting speakers.

Adrian Bell came to Suffolk from London in 1920, aged 19. He was first a farm pupil, then a farmer and lived in various parts of the county for the next 60 years until his death in September 1980. During that time he wrote 25 books, most of which were based on his life and work in Suffolk. His first book was '*Corduroy*', published in 1930. He called the book *Corduroy* because of the clothes the farm workers wore. It describes his early years on the land when farming depended on the horse to do what man could not. '*Silver Ley*' and '*The Cherry Tree*' followed in 1931 and 1932 and completed what has become known as The Trilogy. He also contributed many articles to various magazines, etc. and for 35 years his countryman's notebook was a feature of the Eastern Daily Press (I take this paper on a Saturday just to read his writings which the EDP is now repeating). I love his books and have them all. He was a true Suffolk man who understood the countryside.

The Adrian Bell Society came into being on September 21st, 1996, the aim being to encourage interest in the life and works of Adrian Bell. His books are no longer in print, but to help members, the Society runs a scheme whereby books by A. Bell can be sold to, or bought from other members (or swaps can be arranged). We have a good newsletter twice a year. We also meet twice a year in some village or small town and outings are arranged. We pay £5 a year to be a member and over the years we have had some very good speakers. If you are interested to hear more, contact Mrs M Leighton (Secretary), 3 The Maltings, Church Close, Coltishall, Norwich NR12 7DZ or ring John Ford, Chairman, on 01508 480665.

Hoxne is well known for its St Edmund's Martyrdom in AD 870 although some authorities deny this. The king is said to have sheltered under Goldbrook Bridge and to have been betrayed to the pursuing Danes by a bridal party. Today no girl likes to cross this bridge on her wedding day for fear of bad luck. Liz and I had a good look round Hoxne church which was having a lot of inside work done.

On April 23, my favourite film star and actor, John Mills, died aged 97. He was born in North Elmham and had made so many wonderful films. In April I gave talks at Wickham Market History Society and also at Bildeston. I have got to know Suffolk very well with my talks in villages. Some places I had never heard of before! In May my youngest son, David, phoned me and told me he had been promoted to Police Superintendent. I wished my late husband Ernie (who died in 1980) were alive. He would have been so proud of his two sons, both in the Suffolk police force. I also feel very proud of them, as any mother would. It is the sort of job where when they leave home in the morning you never know if they will return. I always feel a lump in my throat when I hear of a police officer getting killed on duty.

I gave a talk to the W.I. in Ipswich, then in July the country celebrated sixty years since the war ended. There were many celebrations around. In July too I went to the Retirement Club at the ICI Club in Stowmarket. I also did some judging in Alderton. It was this month that my eldest grandchild, Russell, got his degree in Fine Art and Antique Valuation.

I had read in the paper that there was a flower festival

on in Brightwell Church. As it was nearby, off I went. It is a lovely small church and was so well decorated. I get many offers to go and visit various villages. After I had a book from Sid Thurlow, who is in his late eighties telling me about his life in Sapiston near Bury St Edmunds, he invited me to come to lunch and spend the day over there. His daughter Sue said she would meet me half way, as I did not know much about that area. What a day I had. We looked at the church at Sapiston and also at Honington where I met Canon Sally Fogden who does so much for the farming families. I had a lovely day and a cooked lunch with vegetables from Sid's garden.

It was nice meeting Canon Sally Fogden. I had heard a lot about her as she is the local Chaplain to the farming industry. As she was showing me round Honington Church we got talking about Rev. Richard Addington who used to be the Rector of Charsfield. She told me he rang her when the Swine Fever was first confirmed to ask her if there was a fund for farmers. She replied that there was not. "Let's start one," he said. Canon Sally told me she got the ball rolling but called it the Addington Fund as it had been Richard's idea. Within a few days the fund had £1000 in the bank. She had to go to a big agricultural meeting and the farmers were very down. She told them a fund had been started and the whole meeting was lifted, when the farmers realised people were thinking of them. Since the Swine Fever we have had the Foot and Mouth and Blue Tongue diseases so it is a blessing that the Fund was started. It has helped many farming families. The Fund is now run from Stoneleigh Park in Warwickshire.

In September I went to give a talk at Badingham Harvest Festival lunch after the service. The collection was given to me for St Elizabeth's Hospice. My friend Rosemarie Roe had also asked me to go to Shelland to open their Over 60's Sale. It had been a busy weekend. John, my cousin, had brought me some sloes so I made some sloe wine and gin. This is nice drunk in winter when you have a cold. My last talk of the year was at Saxmundham Gardening Club, which was most interesting. A lot of questions were asked. The next thing was the annual Coffee Morning for the Macmillan organisation. I have supported this for years and have always made preserves to sell for this event. I was asked if I would give a talk in Framlingham Church on the making of Akenfield. I have a job to say no, so I gave the talk. On the 25th November George Best died. I am not a football fan but my sons were always talking about him so I knew he was a famous football player. The year finished up with me going to Charsfield to the Over 60's Christmas party. It was so nice to chat with many old friends and neighbours.

The year of 2006 started with a phone call asking if I would be prepared to open a large complex of sheltered homes at Stowupland called '*Steeple View*'. I was collected and taken to have a look at them. They were very nice flats; work was still going on. On February the 9th I was taken there again to do the official opening. There were 100 visitors present. I was asked to plant a tree in front of the flats. I was given a wonderful bouquet of flowers and was then brought home after a very nice tea. It was also this month when one of the biggest bank raids took place in London. There are some awful people around; thank goodness no one was killed. Craig Taylor's new book '*Return to Akenfield*' came out and he had the launch at *The Three Horseshoes* pub in Charsfield.

For some time I had been getting worried about my brother Ronnie as he had told me he had an ulcer on his ankle and that he was cycling twice a week to the doctors' surgery to have it dressed. I asked him to give up his churchyard work and to rest. He had been doing this work and other gardening jobs in the village and had worked so hard all his life. I told him that as he would soon be 70, he should take it easy. However, Ronnie has a will of his own. I know how painful ulcers can be as I had to go into hospital with mine.

Ronnie said he would move to Wickham Market one day but he had said this five or six times before and then had changed his mind. However, he had got his name down for a flat in Wickham Market for when one became vacant. One day he rang me to say his leg was bad and the doctor had told him he may have to go to hospital as he had a hole in his leg. He was worried. I told him I would drive him to see the nurses and doctor. My sister was with me. When Ronnie got into the car he said, "You are never going to believe this but I had the offer of a flat in Wickham Market this morning." I looked at my sister and asked Ronnie what he was going to do about it. He agreed to go and look at it. My sister and I sat in my car while Ronnie saw the doctor. He came out looking as white as a sheet and said he had been told off by the nurses for not resting.

"Come with me," he said, "we will look at this flat."

When he came out he said he would take it. Pat and I looked at each other, amazed;

"Are you sure?" we asked.

He said he could not go on with his leg the way it was. We got back to Charsfield and had a cup of tea and he said I may as well go now. I knew he was in pain but he would not tell anyone about his leg. Ronnie said the worst thing for him was going to be telling his old mate, Bud. Bud lived four doors away and Ronnie would go over to check that he was OK and do odd jobs for him twice a day. For the next two weeks I went over most days and helped Ronnie to pack and to see to all the things you have to do when you move. I knew it was going to be hard on Ronnie, as it had been for me when I had left the village. Ronnie, a bachelor, had been in Charsfield since he was a young boy. The day came for him to move, March the 24th. My sister and brother Peter met him in his new flat and soon got him straight. It would be strange for him but he soon made friends. Ronnie has a heart of gold and will help anyone. It took him over a year to settle down fully and I can understand this as it is a big upheaval. However, his leg was soon improving. We used to visit Charsfield and put flowers on the graves. I dreaded it because as soon as we got to the churchyard Ronnie was worried about the mess and that it was not as he used to keep it. Charsfield had been his life; he liked village life and the nature around him. He drew the covers for the church magazine for some twenty years. He would often ask me for ideas of what to draw.

"Anything to do with the countryside this month" I would say. He is good at drawings and people loved the covers he produced. Ronnie's health has improved and I am sure he did the right thing in moving.

In April I went to Aldeburgh to the Ladies and Gentlemen's Club and also to Leiston Church to talk about the making of Akenfield. It is strange that even after thirty years people still want to hear about how we made the film and all that went on behind the scenes. A friend visited one evening and we got talking about Iken. Daphne told me she had lived in the village. I said I would love to visit the church.

"OK", she said, "we will go."

So off we went. I knew the church had so much history and in 1968 the thatch caught alight and a lot of damage was done. Then a big court case was held in May 1973. The church was roofless for two years as there was a claim that there was no vehicular access to the church and therefore no permission for workmen to pass over Mr G. Clark's property. The court case lasted for 30 days and cost £50,000. The case made legal history when the judge, Mr Justice Megarry, adjourned the hearing to Iken Village Hall for a day to hear evidence. He also attended a mock funeral in which four bearers carried an empty coffin through a gateway to demonstrate the width of access. On July the 26th he rejected the claim by St Edmundsbury and Ipswich Diocesan Board of Finance and Iken Parochial Church Council for orders against Mr Gabriel B. Clark, owner of the adjacent former rectory, requiring him to remove the gates at the southeastern end of the access way from the church lane. It was agreed that Mr Clark was entitled to a declaration that the church could not remove the gates and post without the assent of Mr. Clark or his successors to the ownership of the former rectory. The Rev. Charles Hogwood was rector at the time. He was upset and declined to comment. Mr Clark said he hoped the matter could now be forgotten. He said he knew he had won the court action and that costs had been awarded against the church authorities but there would be no question of he and his wife gloating over the result. What a lot of money it cost the church, I thought, to sort out the access.

The church and the village have been in the news three times. First in the Second World War as in 1942 a total of 650 villagers in Sudbourne and Iken were given 14 days' notice to leave their homes to make way for a wartime battle training ground. Personal belongings could be taken with them but householders had to leave their homes empty, so any furniture that could be removed was placed in storage, sold or simply burnt. The villagers were allowed to return during 1947-48. It must have been an awful time to leave your home, not knowing if you would come back. The second time was after the war. Mr G. Clark and several helpers began to restore the church until it opened its doors again in 1947. Mr Clark was churchwarden then for the third time. Then came the fire in 1968. When clearing the churchyard a spark from the bonfire set fire to the church roof. After all that came the big court case. May the well-known church which looks over the river rest in peace.

The year was progressing and in May my eldest son Allan had completed 32 years in the Suffolk police force so he retired. It was strange to see a photograph in the local papers in which David, my youngest son, was saying goodbye to Allan as he was his boss, which I am sure is unusual. Both my sons had joined as police cadets. Allan's work had been in intelligence and as a detective officer he had good insight into police laws, etc. He had found a new job as a civilian firearm inquiry officer.

Lucy, my youngest granddaughter, gave me an invitation to her dancing club, rather like the Co-op juniors.

They put on a display at the Regent in Ipswich. It was a very good show which involved groups of young people. Most weekends my daughter-in-law Norine and David are running around to take George and Harry to their youth football teams or Lucy to her dancing classes and even girls football matches. Children do have so many opportunities these days. I get used to them saying they are sorry but they can't stop as they're just off to some event or other. It is better than hanging round on the streets.

As the year went on I gave a talk at Gipping Ladies Club and also went to look at the Snape Church exhibition of village life as it used to be. It is fascinating to look at old photos and papers of years gone by. In July BBC television rang me to say the Sunday team of Country File would like to so some filming with me on Akenfield. Therefore, off I went and met the film crew at Hoo Church. Then we went to Letheringham to film the cottage where I lived with my son in the film. There have been many changes in the locality in the last 30 years.

In the August a young girl, Rebecca Rice, was murdered in the nearby village of Pettistree. She was a pretty girl, 18 years old. It appeared that she had moved into a flat there with her boyfriend Stuart Adcock who was charged with her murder. What a waste of young life. Her parents and brothers lived locally at Letheringham where they attended Letheringham church. Later Stuart changed his plea to guilty and is now serving a life sentence. You just don't expect things like this to happen in our small villages. Another shocking event took place later in the year in America when ten little Amish girls were shot in their school. I felt sad about this; it happened in Lancaster, a small town in Pennsylvania that I had visited years before. I have always had a lot of time for these people who lead a quiet life. One thing they do not like is people taking photographs of them so I can imagine how they must have felt when the press and television wanted stories. Charles Roberts had killed the children. He was a milk lorry driver. The Amish do not use machines and farm work is done by hand. There are a few telephones; no televisions and you see them driving round in little buggies with horses. They grieve but do not show angry emotions. It was God's will they said. I was taken round their farms when lecturing in Pennsylvania and I was also shown the wonderful quilts which the women make and sell by the roadside.

The origin of the Amish name comes from their spiritual founder, Jacob Amman of Switzerland who, with a group of followers, separated from the Mennonite movement in 1693, believing the Mennonites had become too liberal. The Amish personality is reserved, modest, calm and quiet. People value obedience to God and their Church. There is simplicity in their manner and lifestyle. They believe in adult baptism and the confession of sins. Most Amish people reject the majority of modern technology but not all. For instance, the Amish are not permitted to own cars but they are allowed to ride in cars owned by non-Amish individuals for travel to faraway funerals or for important errands. They also make similar provisions with telephones. They may sometimes use them to conduct important business or to make contact with a relative but none are allowed inside the home. It is not the technology that the Amish people reject; it is the baggage the technology brings. A phone in the house would open their ideas to invasion from the outside world. Using a public phone is okay but a quiet family could easily be interrupted by the jangling ring of a phone if it were permitted in the home.

The Amish travel around in horse-drawn buggies. You see them going up and down the road with big lorries passing them. The horses don't seem to mind the traffic. One Amish lady told me what her day was like. Most get up at 4 a.m.; yes 4 a.m! The men go to milk the cows, feed the horses and the rest of the stock. At 5 a.m., the family sit round for breakfast. Her son leaves for work at 5.30 a.m. By 6.30 a.m. Emma (a daughter) helps with the ironing, then they go outside to plant sweet corn and peppers. At 7.30 a.m. they clean and tidy the

house as it was used for a Church service the day before.
At 8.30 a.m. they get the horse and buggie ready to visit
another daughter five miles away to help clean her house. She
and her husband have just moved in. At 2.30 p.m. they return
home. She must do the washing, then the cooking for the
evening meal. Her husband and son come home from the
fields at 5.30 p.m. to milk and feed the stock. At 7 p.m. the
family sits down for a family meal. At 9.00 p.m. evening
prayers are said and everyone is ready for bed.

On some days they will have singing at their home
with up to 100 visitors, they will feed them all. When I was in
Pennsylvania I noticed what good cooks they were. We had a
meal in an Amish restaurant; the food was good and home-
cooked.

We also stayed with an Amish family for bed and
breakfast, starting with prayers, a nice cooked breakfast and
returning in the evening for a good meal. Then we had more
prayers and were left to do as we wished. The lady would chat
but the husband was out on his farm. We were surprised to
find the Amish family running the bed and breakfast but, as
the wife explained to us, some things are changing and they
could see no harm in giving rest and food. Some families
would not do this she told us. But we enjoyed two nights with
them and found them charming people. Whenever we stopped
by the roadside to see the quilts, they made you so welcome
and you were soon asked into their homes. I have a lot of time
for the Amish people.

I still get many calls asking if there is a video of
'*Akenfield*' and I can reply that it is now available, but only
on DVD. One day Mr Terry Mott rang me to ask where he
could get one. You will remember I have spoken about him as
he was the cancer consultant at Ipswich Hospital who looked
after me. Once he retired he moved to a farmhouse in a village
nearby, with a garden, orchards and buildings. I told him I
would take him a DVD. A nice cup of tea is always offered
when you visit their home and we always have a laugh. He

grows good vegetables too.

On October the 10th Russell started work at Neal, Sons and Fletcher Estate Agents, Auctioneers and Valuers in Woodbridge after gaining his degree in Fine Art and Antique Valuation. I was sure he would be happy there as they are a well-known firm and very friendly people. Thank God he has a job; so many young people who do their time at university, come home and can't find a job.

When I first went to see the saleroom where Russell worked and did the auctions, I had to find out about the history of the place as it was not like other salerooms. I discovered that it was once a theatre owned by David Fisher in October 1813. It was originally part of The Angel public house, sometimes known as The Black Boar. The owner at that time was Mr George Brook-Keer. The shape of the building was influenced by the lack of road frontage to the site, hence the long passageway leading from Bridewell Street (the former name for Theatre Street) to a rectangular area of land measuring about 100ft by 32ft.

The present car park was formerly occupied by a terrace of cottages facing the road. The theatre, holding up to 80 people, was built by Mr Thompson for a total cost of £2000 and was opened on Saturday 5 February 1814. The Fisher Company Theatre held performances there until 1844. Ownership had changed in March 1833 to Thomas Saddler, a Norwich grocer, and the late Benjamin Moulton who was an auctioneer. The building carried on as a theatre until 1861. Then in 1862 the premises were purchased to be used as a national school and the building was extended and modified. It was sold by auction in 1962 at the Crown Hotel in Woodbridge to Doctor Littler. Then later again the building was acquired by the late Dennis H. B. Neal and was used as the Theatre Street saleroom for many years. This activity still continues today as the building has been passed to his sons. It is well worth a visit; sales are held monthly. It is one of the most fascinating small buildings in Woodbridge.

From Akenfield to Pastures New

I went to Hasketon Women's Institute 60th birthday party. They are a group of kind ladies and they always make me feel welcome. One lady picks me up for meetings as I no longer like driving at night. The car lights seem to dazzle me with their brightness.

One thing I do miss in my bungalow is cupboard space. I had been thinking for weeks that I must get rid of my slides and transparencies as I have so many, in fact thousands. I thought a charity may like them, so I put an advertisement in a local paper saying, 'Free to a good home, slides of countryside views, flowers and animals.' I had one gentleman ring me and say he would take them and give them to good homes such as the Royal Horticultural Society as there were so many slides of flowers and shrubs for example. I hated parting with them but I knew my family would not know what to do with them later on. I gave some to the Suffolk Record Office as I had taken one slide of every house in Charsfield and this could be a record of history in time. I have also stated that when I pass on, all my slides of Akenfield are to go to the Suffolk Record Office. Over the years I have travelled many thousands of miles giving illustrated talks but now I feel that it's time to give up because of my arthritis.

The December of that year did not end well for our local town, Ipswich. My son David was in charge of the Zest nightclub shooting case. It seems to have been a terrifying gangland-style shooting. There were six shots, one fatal, inside the nightclub in the early hours of December the 8th. Up to 800 people were in the club and many fled through fire exits. Then to crown it, Ipswich was once more put on the map when, over a period of time, five prostitutes were found dead. Steve Wright was arrested and charged. The trial was due to start in January 2008. You will think that these last few pages have been all about awful killings. Who would have thought this could happen in our area? Suffolk has always been known as quiet and slow. And I may as well tell you that at the end of this month Saddam Hussein was hanged.

January 2007 was not so good for me as I had chest pains once more so was given more antibiotics. As I have said, I don't like the early winter months. This must have been the first time that I had not bought any Seville oranges since way back in the early 1950's when I made my first batch of marmalade. I used to buy them by the case and I have made thousands of pounds of marmalade for W.I. markets and charity stalls over the years. My brother used to spend many hours helping me to cut oranges by hand. Now my hands are getting more painful with the arthritis and Carpal tunnel syndrome in my right hand. So I had to resist buying any Sevilles which I can tell you made me rather sad.

In the February there was an outbreak of bird flu at a Bernard Matthews turkey farm at Halesworth. Poultry farmers can never tell when this is going to happen to them. We also had snow in February, not very much but we were told that schools would have to close. Why is it that when we get a little snow in this country everything comes to a standstill? When we were children and had three or four feet of snow our schools never closed. We just walked to school and got there the best way we could. I invited my friend Roy Tricker to lunch. We always have a good 'mardel' and Roy will tell me the history of the churches on my postcards. He knows so much about churches and gives very good lectures all over the country. His humour is a joy to listen to.

In March my grandson Russell got his first little house in Melton so I enjoyed going to see this and the garden, which is very small but I am sure he will manage to run it well. A local village pub was also opened again. This was the Blaxhall Ship. There had been a lot of publicity about this as the village had wanted it to be re-opened. At one time it was so well known for its old time country singing, music and step dancing and from what I hear it has been doing very well since re-opening. In April we heard of another shooting in Virginia, USA. A man shot 32 young students in a school. This sort of thing seems to be happening a lot today.

At this time of the year I enjoy having a few hours in my greenhouse to sow a few seeds. It's surprising what vegetables you can grow in pots and I also experiment with planting vegetables in my flower borders, like spinach, Swiss chard, beetroot and parsley. The flowers mix well with the foliage. "Where there's a will, there's a way," I am told.

We didn't have any rain in April 2007 and I had to water the pots early in the year as the plants were drying out. This was unusual for this time of year. In May I went to give a talk at Stowmarket for the Salvation Army. I still go to press days for the Suffolk Show. It's nice to meet old friends and you do have the opportunity to be able to write about new events and any changes that are going to take place at the Show. In May I was told that my great aunt Phyllis Butters had died. She was 89 and had lived in a residential flat in Needham Market. She was such a cheerful lady. We would often have chats on the telephone and she told me so much about my late grandmother and the family (friends have been helping me to do my family tree). Aunt Phil, as I called her, gave me so much information. She was only partially sighted but she never grumbled. I do miss our little chats.

Friends rang me to ask if I had seen the Suffolk magazine for that month as I had been chosen as one of fifty interesting women in Suffolk. I felt rather embarrassed. As I have said many times, I am just a country girl. I suppose I have had more opportunities than many but I still feel that I am an ordinary country person.

On the May Bank Holiday it was the first time in sixty years that the Framlingham Gala had to be cancelled; this was due to heavy rain. Many other events had to be cancelled too. In June I went with friends to Waldringfield Church as the Rev. John Waller was celebrating 150 years of the Waller family serving Waldringfield, Hemley and Newbourne churches and villages. This must be a record for the diocese. A friend asked me if I would like a ticket for Woodbridge Flower Club as it was celebrating its fifty-fifth birthday. I was an early member - I used to go in 1959 and enjoy the flower demonstrations and take part in the monthly competitions.

Late May is when I like to put my hanging baskets out, hoping for no more frost. This is one job I love. I always do four for my youngest son David and four baskets of fuchsias for Allan. I have been doing this for years. Then I do five for myself, it gives me a lot of pleasure. Each year as I start on the patio pots Allan will say, "Don't forget, Mum, they'll all need water and the drier the summer, the more watering you will have to do."

Most baskets are bought ready-planted, usually on impulse in the spring when colourful displays can be seen hanging up in garden centres everywhere. The baskets are usually made up of strong wire but plastic ones used as salad shakers are suitable, though less durable. The soil is kept in place by lining the inside of the basket with moss. If moss is not easily obtainable, black polythene makes an adequate substitute (I use one of the 80 litre bags I buy my compost in and turn it inside out). Get a large pot to stand your basket in, or an old bucket will do as this gives you room to work all round the basket. You need to have plants at almost flowering size before the basket is hung up. Meanwhile it can stand on the empty pot or bucket.

You can plant all sorts of trailing varieties in the basket. Lobelia, ivy leaf geraniums, pendulous begonias, fuchsias and petunias are among the most satisfactory. I also like to put some vegetables like tumbler tomatoes in baskets with two or three roots of parsley and a root of chives in the middle of the basket. For years I used to go to the Press Day at the Chelsea Flower Show and over the years I have seen many good ideas. When I used to go and look at the hanging basket stands there would sometimes be up to one hundred hanging baskets with all sorts of flowers, herbs and vegetables. For years I have loved making up baskets and I love to see them hanging on houses and shops. I have an iron stand in my front garden which takes four baskets. For the last two years I have planted them up with pendulous begonia in vibrant yellow and orange colours. They make a wonderful show.

However, I must tell you a hanging basket will take a lot of water (twice a day in very hot weather). In addition, you do need good compost. I always have a bag of good farm muck bought from friends so I start with good drainage in the bottom, then a layer of muck (this must be a year old, do not use new muck of any sort as it gets hot and burns the roots). If you have no muck, mix some slow release fertilizer in. You can also use water holding granules in with the compost but not all experts agree. I used to have a water tank with half a sack of muck soaking in the water. Then my brother Ronnie used to feed all my baskets and containers with this feed. My eldest son still feeds his baskets and pots in this way. Many people think that if it rains there will be no need to water but don't you believe it. The rain will only run off as the soil and roots soon get very packed together and they need a good soak. So if you want a good basket, be prepared to look after it.

I felt rather upset in the June as I had to have my late husband's ring cut off my finger because of the Carpal tunnel syndrome in my right hand. With the arthritis too my hand was painful and swollen and the ring had become tight. In June I was asked to go back to Charsfield to open the fête in aid of St Peter's Church. The day was cold and wet. The fête was held in the church secretary's garden. Times have changed since the village fête was held in rectory gardens. Nowadays so many rectories have been sold off so you have to hold these events where you can. It had been six years since I had left the village and there were so many new faces. Villages of today soon change with new people moving in. I was able to tell Ronald Blythe (I call him Ronnie) about the fête as in the following fortnight Roy Tricker picked me up and took me to have lunch with Ronnie. He made us so welcome. I had been to see him many times but it was Roy's first visit. The weather was fine and the scenery so lovely. It was nice being a passenger so I could look around. We looked at Ronnie's garden and then he gave us a very good lunch and we chatted. As Roy serves in the church, Ronnie and he had a lot to talk about. Roy got me home safely. We had been having a lot of thunderstorms so we were lucky to pick a good day to see Ronnie. Yorkshire was having the worst of the rain and we saw on the television many homes flooded out. How dreadful to lose all your special photos, books and personal goods. Furniture you can replace but not personal pieces.

Mr Tony Blair stepped down from his job of Prime Minister. I wondered what would happen now with the government. It was also noted that this June had been the wettest on record and we were not even finished with the

Woodbridge Tide Mill - Just down the road

month yet. For the first time since I had lived in Melton, I saw my garden under water. There was so much rain during the summer - not much fun for people on holiday. You saw people at the seaside looking miserable with their raincoats on. It's rotten if you have small children and they can't go and play in the sand! And for some more miserable news, foot and mouth disease had reared its ugly head again. It had been six years since the previous outbreak. I hoped we were not going to see the large fires and animals burning once more. An awfully worrying time for farmers again.

I was so pleased to hear that my granddaughter Sarah had passed her Law with German degree. She was having her graduation in Birmingham this month. I would have loved to have seen her graduate but I know there would have been a lot of people about and tickets were limited to two per family. Sarah has not yet finished with her law studies as she is one of the lucky ones to have a job lined up; with Birketts solicitors in Ipswich but she has to go and do another year's study at law school in York and pass more exams. She has worked very hard.

I was collected one day in August and taken to open John Coles' farm shop at '*Roselea Nursery*' in Kirton near Trimley St. Martin. I have known John since we did gardening programmes together on the radio. He has a wonderful nursery, very much a family concern, growing vegetables, salads, cut flowers, bedding plants, etc, and the shop sells pet foods, fresh fruit, free range eggs, etc. He also does local deliveries. I was very impressed with the whole day out and as is the case with many more people, it's hard work that has got the family and staff where they are today.

On September the 6th I heard that Luciano Pavarotti had died. He had sung in all the great opera houses all over the world. I loved his singing; he was, I am sure, the greatest opera singer of our time. Many people were sad to hear of his death. Also this month we saw another disease hit the farmers; this time it was 'blue tongue disease'. This has been known to affect cattle in overseas countries but it was the first outbreak in Britain. It seemed that the 'midge' mosquito-like insect bit the cattle and it's thought that they come into the country when the weather gets warm. I hoped it would not get as bad as the Foot and Mouth outbreaks.

I took a ride to see my old neighbour Alan Spicer, who used to be headmaster at Kingston School in Woodbridge which is now gone and The Grove residential home has been built in its place. Alan and Amy, his wife lived nearly next door to my old home and had fruit orchards. When Alan retired he often used to come in and see me. I had a gate at the top of the garden into his orchard. He would come to see when I was planting seeds or taking cuttings, so then he would go home and do the same. Sometimes he came in for coffee and cake. When his wife Amy retired, they bought a barn at Badingham and made it into a lovely home. Then Amy died. Poor Alan was devastated; they had had so much planned for their retirement. Alan and I started to go out for visits to churches. He was a good organist and used to play at St Peter's, Charsfield. After a while I noticed that Alan was having a job to remember where we were going on some days when we had arranged to visit some church or other. After a time he moved into a smaller house at Laxfield. I rang his daughter to see how he was and asked if I could call in. He was so pleased to see me but he was so confused. It made me very sorry to see him like this as he used to be very intelligent. I am sure he still is but his memory was going. I told him I was going back to Hoo church for their harvest service. He asked me ten times where I was going. It is sad when you see this happening to people you know so well. I drove on to have a cup of tea with my old friends David and Margaret Doe and after a good chat with Margaret I then went to the harvest service at Hoo. Margaret and Perry are the churchwardens. I do not know what this small village would do without them. If they gave up I think the church would close. The preacher was the Rev. John Berg who had retired from Japan and lived in Melton. He told us he had been a minister in Japan for many years. He was most interesting; he had seen a lot of trouble out there. As I came home it made me count my blessings.

My camera had packed up so my granddaughter Sarah suggested I buy a digital one. I did not think I would get used to it but after a time I enjoyed using it. I have to get used to all this technology, as my grandchildren tell me.

Chapter 8

Suffolk Churches

The year was going so quickly; I think we notice this happening as we get older. In October John and Audrey took me to visit Damsden St. Andrew church near Needham Market. This is a church I had had on my list to visit for a long time. It was up a long lane, nearly a mile off the main road. It is such a quiet and peaceful spot with wonderful views across Gipping, Creetings and Shrubland Park. It is a tiny building. It was declared redundant in 1979 but the good people of the parish bought the church and formed the St Andrew's trust. There is now a service once a month. On the door is a poem that I liked:

Now the little church is up for sale
Some folks say, "Well, it's getting old"
But others say, "Yes, so it might be,
But we'll fight like mad to keep it free."
It's so beautiful to close for ever
When so many friends get together
Once a month on a Sunday afternoon
To say a prayer and sing a hymn
And thank the Lord for everything."

Everything is small in scale, that's what I liked about it but I could not get over how well kept it was. It's a credit to the Damsden people. There is so much I could write about this dear little church and I would recommend a visit. Roy Tricker tells me he always takes the Rogation Service there each year.

After my visit to Damsden Church, I thought a lot about our churches of Suffolk. My friend Roy Tricker has a huge knowledge of churches and has written so many histories of churches and church guides.

Some people will tell you Suffolk is an odd place, a landscape of wide, coastal marshes and big inland horizons on the Norfolk border. Many of our Suffolk churches were rebuilt in the 15th Century. But as we can see, the village or town church still stands despite all the happenings over the years. Ipswich has twelve medieval churches still standing, which must be a record. Some of the largest churches in Suffolk are Lavenham, Blythburgh, Long Melford and Southwold, all to do with the wool trade in the past. Some of the most interesting churches are in Dennington and Kedington in the west part of Suffolk. No doubt you will think your village church is the most interesting. Perhaps it is to you, and why not? To me any church is a wonderful place. How did people all those years ago manage to build such wonderful places without all the technology of today?

In the November bird flu was confirmed at Palgrave near Diss. This was another worry for poultry dealers just before Christmas. The birds were farmed out to farmers who have spare buildings and yards. The owners were the Buchanan family from Debach, only a few miles from Melton. I know the family and felt so sorry for them as thousands of turkeys had to be killed. December finished up with the assassination in Pakistan of the 54 year old former Prime Minster Benazir Bhutto.

The new year did not start too well as I went down with a flu-like illness. I had had the jab the previous October so it couldn't have been flu but there were a lot of strange illnesses about at this time. It took three weeks for me to feel like my old self again. Sitting in my armchair I had a call from a reporter at the East Anglian Daily Times asking me if I could tell him a bit of history on the only thatched cottage in Charsfield as it was about to come on the market. He wanted to know if there had ever been a shop there and any other history about it. As I told him, I had only lived in the village for forty-one years and there hadn't been a shop at 'The Thatch' in my time but before then, who knows? It is a very old and very pretty cottage.

Robert Blake, a well known author from Woodbridge,

called to see me bringing his latest book of photography on Woodbridge. My brother Ronnie had not been too well and I had told him to go and see the doctor. He rang me to tell me he had got shingles, which is a nasty complaint. It came as a shock to him. I told him to rest and keep warm but I am afraid Ronnie has a will of his own. I made him some Shepherd's pie and advised him to eat plenty of fruit so he could get some Vitamin C. The month of January was very mild and it turned out to be the warmest on record.

Another friend, Michael, called to see me. He keeps many pretty varieties of chickens and he brought me a box of really brown free-range eggs. They were the colour of chocolate. I used to keep Maran chickens which lay these nice dark eggs. He also brought me a pot of aconites to plant and a shrub called Sarcococca (Buxaceae), sometimes called Christmas or Sweet Box. The perfumed white flowers on dark glossy leaves just filled my conservatory with a wonderful scent which was welcome in the dark winter months. More friends called - Eric and Perry - with a bag of root vegetables. Eric is a very good gardener and has garden greenhouses plus an allotment. My son had also brought me a brace of pheasant so I was able to make some good winter soups. I also had a chat with Max Pemberton who used to live in Charsfield. I knew his family very well. Max was a well known solicitor in Woodbridge until he retired and he had also completed a book about his life and living in Charsfield. He had lent me a copy to read just before Christmas and I did enjoy it. I rang to thank him and he told me to keep the book so I shall be able to let other people who know Max read it. I know it will bring back many memories to older residents.

As the weeks slipped by many people were following the trial of Steve Wright, aged 49, and the murder of the 5 prostitutes in Ipswich. I had looked on my computer each day and followed the case, keeping a record of the day's events. This went on for six weeks. Then on February the 21st he was found guilty of murdering all five women. It only took six hours for the jury of nine men and three women to find him guilty. Thank goodness for DNA as this was crucial in this case. Over six weeks in December 2006 Steve Wright had killed five prostitutes and dumped their bodies in streams and on wasteland on the outskirts of Ipswich. This really had shaken the people of Ipswich and in fact people all over the country and he has gone down as one of the notorious killers of our time.

We in Suffolk couldn't believe it could happen here. All the local and national newspapers were full of it. I have built up a large scrapbook about these Suffolk murders as I thought someone may like to read it in years to come.

My New Back Garden

Chapter 9

Around Woodbridge

I said at the beginning of this book how I would miss seeing the barn owl flying low over the field in front of my old home. However, I should not complain as there are some very nice sights around this area. My son Allan has always told me of the pretty walks along the river which is only a little way from my home. You just have to cross the railway line and you are into the boat yard. As you walk you can turn left and walk towards Wilford Bridge; from here you can then walk towards Sutton Hoo, the site of the greatest archaeological find ever made or ever likely to be made in England. I have heard it said that if you live near to a well known sight or house, you never seem to visit it. The visitors are people who have come a long way. I have never done this particular walk; it's too long for me now but I can walk and sit on the seats along the river wall and watch birds like avocets and oyster catchers. My daughter-in-law, Jackie, has seen kingfishers near the river. There is a good view across the river looking towards Sutton Hoo.

I can't imagine what Mr Basil Brown must have thought when he was working and opening some of the burrows in 1938. He discovered a great ship, much of which had rotted away. It was rumoured to be a Viking ship burial of the ninth or tenth century. A great hoard of treasure was found which included gold, bronze and silver. It must have been a royal grave and it was thought to have been Raedwald, King of all East Anglia. The treasure was taken out carefully and sent to the British Museum Laboratory. A fine helmet had been found but it was damaged with the collapse of the burial chamber, which one can imagine with the decomposed timber. The gold items and the jewellery had kept well. It must have been overwhelming to find all this treasure. People now come from all over to see the fine display of replicas on view. Only recently, since I moved to Melton, the National

Trust has opened a brand new exhibition hall to display their discoveries. In the summer the roads are busy with traffic leading to Sutton Hoo.

Then on the same road there is Hollesley Bay, worth a visit in your car, not to see the well known prison but to look at the Suffolk horse - the Suffolk Punch. There are only 300 of these horses remaining in this country, fewer than the giant panda and the Siberian tiger. It is truly an endangered species and now their survival is critical. When Hollesley Bay Prison was set to sell its farm and the Suffolk horse stud, the Suffolk Punch Trust was formed and by March 2006 the £700,000 required to buy the stud and the 188 acres had been raised. The Suffolk Punch had been on the site for over 250 years. Fundraising is now going on to open a village centre and museum. It is worth riding round the roads and seeing the horses, some with their young, in the meadows. I remember last year I drove to Shingle Street with my brother. We were so pleased to see the mothers and their young foals in the meadows. I stopped the car and we got out and stood near the gate watching them. It was a real treat.

Now back to walking from Melton. If you turn right at the boat yard you can, if you are fit, walk right through to Martlesham Creek. The first time I walked along the path looking across the Deben Estuary with the boat houses along the pathway, I had my son's dog Megan with me (she loved the river). I was delighted to see one houseboat with pots of plants around the boat. There was so much colour in the containers of all sizes and even the bank had been planted. Woodbridge holds a good maritime event each year. This includes special activities on the river and it gives great pleasure to many people. It is all free to watch.

You can keep walking along the river to Kyson Point but if you want to look in at Woodbridge you will come to the Old Tide Mill. I am sure Woodbridge people must feel very proud of this as a lot of time, effort and money has been spent on the mill. I understand that from Easter 2008 it will be working to show how flour is made from wheat. Also you will be able to buy flour to make your bread and cereals for breakfast. There is an art club near the mill with local artists' work on sale. Close by is the railway station. I have chatted to many visitors who have told me they love coming to Woodbridge, a splendid little Georgian country town. The Shire Hall was built by Thomas Seckford in 1570. It has two floors and the top one was once used as a court room (we used to have a saying, "it will cost you a shilling a step to go into that room"). Now for the time being it is used as the Suffolk Punch Heavy Horse Museum. There is a wonderful collection of historic photographs and family mementoes and silverware. The ground floor is used by the local council. Just across the road is the Woodbridge Museum, which tells the whole story of the town up to the present day and just behind the museum stands St Mary's Church. Then walking up Market Hill to your right past the Shire Hall along the road for about 15 minutes, you will see Buttrum's Mill. This is a magnificent windmill, a six storey red brick tower mill with white sails and fan wheel. You don't see many like this in the countryside today. It is open on Sundays and Bank Holidays from May to September.

I feel lucky to be living near to this little town. It has a lot to offer and the charm is that there are still small shops. There are plenty of restaurants along and near the Thoroughfare. You have Gobbitts Yard where there is an assortment of small shops. There are four book shops, two bakers, where fresh bread is made six days a week, and there is also a farmers' market held in the Community Hall next to the swimming pool on the second and fourth Saturdays of each month. I help with the Country Market held every Thursday from 10.00 to 11.15 a.m. in the same hall. This used to be known all over the country as the Women's Institute market but now the name has changed. We sell home-made cakes, preserves, eggs, cards, crafts, plants, flowers and vegetables. You can also meet friends there and have a coffee and a scone.

In Woodbridge there is plenty of self-catering, bed and breakfast and hotel accommodation. We are very fortunate to have so many places of interest to visit in the area - Framlingham Castle and Orford Castle for example. Seckford Hall is worth visiting for its excellent food and accommodation. It is on the outskirts of Woodbridge. Snape Maltings is famous for its beautiful setting and is so well known for its festivals and concerts. It was made famous by Benjamin Britten. Leiston has the Long Shop Museum. This was once the Garrett Works, It now houses steam rollers and other machines used in peaceful times, as well as tanks and shells used in war. The remains of Leiston Abbey can also be seen. The Lady Chapel is the only complete building left of the grand church and if you want to see Sizewell, Britain's largest atomic power station, this is also close to Leiston.

Just up the road from there is Minsmere, the wonderful place where people flock to see birdlife and wild flowers. There are many miles of wet lands and open countryside. Easton Farm Park is only a fifteen minute drive from where I live and is a good place to take young children to see baby animals. You can take nice walks there too. Ten minutes from Easton Farm Park is Hoo Church where we filmed scenes from '*Akenfield*'. I am often asked which church was used in the film so I thought I would add this. The sites I have mentioned are all less than a fl hour drive from Woodbridge. There are so many places of interest near this little town.

I have now been in my new home for seven years. When I first moved to Melton I never thought that I would ever feel at home in the same way as I had at Charsfield, however I can honestly now say I have never been more contented, especially when I am sitting in my little office, surrounded by my books, looking out of my window and enjoying my hobbies which I have had to put on one side for so long.

COUNCIL HOUSE
GARDEN
ADMISSION 20P